Do-It-All-Yourself Needlepoint

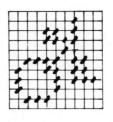

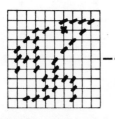

Original designs by
Marjorie Sablow

Photographs by
Eugene Sablow

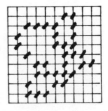

DO-IT-ALL-YOURSELF
YOURSELF
NEEDLEPOINT

by Joan Scobey and
Lee Parr McGrath

AN ESSANDESS ® SPECIAL EDITION   NEW YORK

DO-IT-ALL-YOURSELF NEEDLEPOINT

SBN: 671-10617-1

Copyright © 1971 by Joan Scobey and Lee Parr McGrath.

Illustrations copyright © 1971, by Simon & Schuster, Inc.

All rights reserved. Published by ESSANDESS SPECIAL EDITIONS,

a division of Simon & Schuster, Inc., 630 Fifth Avenue,

New York, N.Y. 10020.

Printed in the U.S.A.

Second Printing

Designed by The Etheredges

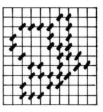

Contents

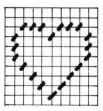

Acknowledgments

Our appreciation goes to Dorothy Perkins, of The Knitting Needle, Armonk, N.Y., for her invaluable assistance; to The Embroiderers' Guild; Al Mintz, of Mazaltov's, Inc.; Charles Quaintance, of Alice Maynard; The Friends of Art, Kansas City, Mo.; to the staff of the Mamaroneck Free Library, especially Mrs. Lola Dudley and Miss Miriam Baumann; and to Marti Huber, Laura Cadwallader, Monica Meenan, Clarice Adee, and Mrs. Zelda Levine.

Grateful thanks are also due to the following needle-pointers who graciously loaned their work or stitched designs from this book for the photographs: Mrs. Abbie J. Blum, Mrs. Elliott Coulter, Mrs. John M. Friedman, Mrs. Richard S. Fuld, Mrs. Allan Gevertz, Mrs. Allan Harvey, Mrs. Warren Heilbron, Mrs. Michael Hessberg, Mrs. Herbert Hirschfeld, Mrs. Joseph Mintzer, Mrs. Lewis Myers, Mrs. Nat Myers, Mrs. Oscar Sachs, and Mrs. Leonard Steiner.

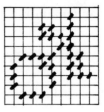

Introduction

The joys of needlepoint are for Everywoman. This simple pastime offers a rich diversity of delights to suit every temperament. And those who try stitching a canvas usually discover that, like eating peanuts, it's impossible to stop.

A piece of needlepoint is an agreeable companion, either restful or challenging to suit your moods. An intricate pattern or complex shape will hold your attention to the exclusion of tensions or worries. Covering large background areas, on the other hand, is pleasantly soothing when you are alone, a welcome contrast to the hectic pace of most of our lives, and undemanding enough to combine well with sociable conversation.

As lagniappe, needlepoint is transportable. Tucked into a small space, it is conveniently at hand to wile away long car trips, a train commute, or waits for the car pool. It fits handily into those odd bits of spare time interspersed through a woman's day.

For those who enjoy crafts, but not the cleaning up, working with yarn and needle is delightfully neat. No messy paint brushes, scraps of fabrics, spills of glue. For those who like to be in good company, needlepoint is a hobby to share with Princess Grace, Joanne Woodward, Julie Eisenhower, and the Duke and Duchess of Windsor, among others.

On a deeper level, needlepoint is a protest against automation and technocracy. In homes that of necessity contain much that is mass-produced, stitchery is a touch of hand-crafted warmth. By transforming canvas, yarn, and your ideas into beautiful and useful objects that will last for generations, you will achieve—and deserve—a satisfying glow of good husbandry.

Expressing your own individuality and creativity is, of course, the ultimate pleasure in needlepoint. And this book is written to help you do just that—to design, stitch, finish, and mount your own ideas. It provides all the information a beginner needs, as well as some tips for the more experienced. It will help you thread your way through available yarns, canvases, supplies, and suppliers.

Most important to you, this book includes a 51-page section of pattern components, with which you can create and transfer to canvas professional designs exactly as you would like them. You needn't have any artistic talent to use these pattern elements; they are traceable and are already on grids if you want to count meshes. They will combine in an almost infinite variety of patterns to suit your personal taste, whether for op, pop, paisley, or peonies. Try them and you will discover that putting your own design on canvas is the way to twice the fun and half the cost.

Taste the delights of needlemania and add a diverting and enriching interest to your life. To do it easily and inexpensively, follow this guide to do-it-all-yourself needlepoint.

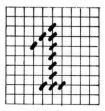

What You Need to Begin

Needlepoint equipment is easily assembled and reasonable in cost. (If you are not near a needlepoint shop, a list of mail order sources is on page 177).

CANVAS

Needlepoint canvas, commonly of cotton, is woven to form regular squares and is stiffened with sizing for body and stitching ease. It is described in meshes, or squares per inch. Thus, No. 10 canvas has ten holes, or meshes, per inch; No. 5 canvas has five meshes per inch. It is woven in a variety of mesh sizes, ranging from coarse canvas of three and four meshes per inch to canvas of thirty-two and forty meshes per inch, which is so fine that it is almost indistinguishable from fabric.

There are two basic types of canvas. Mono, or single thread, canvas is usually white. It is an excellent background for painting designs and for counting stitches. When buying it, look for a glossy rather than pasty look; the highly polished threads will take more abuse.

Penelope, or double thread, canvas is woven with two threads for each mesh. It is a little harder to use at first than mono because the threads are not evenly spaced; the pair of vertical threads are woven close to each other, and the horizontal threads are more widely spaced (see photograph on page 16). The great advantage of penelope canvas is that it can be split for finer work in detailed areas of the design, such as faces or lettering, or for occasional changes in pattern. You simply spread both the horizontal and vertical double threads apart to form four smaller meshes where before there was only a large one. The double weave also locks the canvas in place, making it more stable than mono canvas and permitting some stitches not possible on mono canvas.

Unless you need areas of smaller—petit point—stitches in your canvas, work with mono. In most canvas sizes penelope is harder to stitch because the double thread makes the working mesh smaller, therefore it's harder to pull the needle through and the work goes twice as slow. The double weave is also harder to cover in Gobelin, Bargello, or any of the vertical stitches.

When selecting your canvas, weigh the amount of detail you want to include against the time and patience you want to invest in the piece. Every time you go to a smaller mesh, you increase the number of required stitches, and hence your time investment.

No. 10 MONO is excellent for most needlepoint and particularly good for beginners. It will allow you to finish a project in reasonable time and, although you can't catch fine detail, you will be able to stitch fairly intricate shapes. For more detail or shading, use No. penelope, or go to No. 12, No. 14, or finer mono canvas.

No. 5 PENELOPE was originally used for rugs, and still is, but it has also become a popular mesh for quickly working up pillows and other accessories in bold, simple designs. The slanting stitches cover it well, and it has even spawned a new stitch called "quick point" (see p. 18).

No. 12 MONO is a good size canvas to use for vertical stitches like Gobelin. Bargello, or brick. The same weight wool that you use for needlepointing on No. 10 mono will cover nicely for Bargello work on No. 12 mono. The reason you need either a smaller mesh or heavier yarn is that the stitches run vertically rather than diagonally, and therefore need to be fuller to cover the canvas adequately.

WOVEN CANVAS is triple thick, eight meshes to the inch, with a pattern actually woven into the canvas.

It is available in a variety of patterns, and you use cross stitch or half cross stitch to work the pattern. Any other stitch makes the backing too thick.

YARN

A wealth of yarns and threads are available for needlepointing. The only requirement is that the yarn cover the canvas and be durable enough to withstand both the abrasion of stitching and any wear and tear the finished piece might get. Coarse canvas with fewer meshes per square inch requires thick yarn, and as the number of mesh per square inch increases, thinner and thinner yarns may be used.

Most yarns are colorfast and mothproof. They differ mainly in their weight, the number of plies (the strands making up the thread), and how tightly those plies are twisted together in the yarn. Whatever yarn you use, always try to buy enough for your project—particularly for the background—and note the manufacturer and color or dye lot number for all wool. Figure 1 shows various canvases with appropriate yarns.

TAPESTRY WOOL is four-ply yarn that comes in matched dye lots and an adequate range of colors (over fifty in most brands). It is excellent for No. 10 canvas. It cannot be split for use on finer mesh, but it can be doubled for coarser canvas.

PERSIAN WOOL is two-ply wool sold in three-thread strands that can be worked separately or together. It is sold by the skein, the ounce, and even by the strand in some stores and is available in an enormous range of colors and shades. It is a sturdy yarn that has a slightly luminous quality, which adds depth. Use the full three strands on No. 10 canvas; one strand if you are splitting No. 10 penelope into smaller squares; two of the three strands (or one strand doubled) on No. 12 or No. 14 canvas; one full strand doubled (six threads) on No. 7 canvas; eight strands on No. 5 penelope.

KNITTING WORSTED is four-ply wool that can't be easily separated. It is cheaper than tapestry or Persian wools, but is less durable and comes in fewer colors. Use it on No. 10 canvas.

RUG WOOL is three-ply, rougher textured yarn. Use it on No. 8 canvas or lower.

In addition to these basic yarns for covering the

Figure 1.–From left: No. 5 penelope with rug wool, 8 strands Persian wool, 3 strands tapestry wool; No. 10 penelope then No. 10 mono, each with knitting worsted, tapestry wool and 3 strands Persian wool; No. 12 mono with tapestry wool and 2 strands Persian wool.

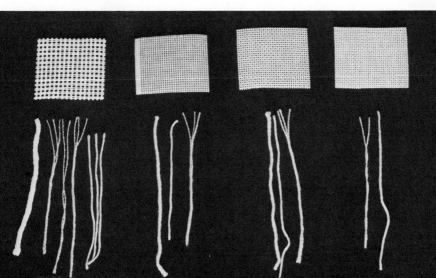

canvas, you can use a greater variety of accent yarns for special effects—embroidery cotton, pearl cotton, silks, metallic threads, linen threads, Lurex mixtures, string, and raffia. They are usually embroidered over already stitched needlepoint rather than directly onto the canvas. They are not durable but perform well to accent highlights, put a gleam in an eye or in other unexpectedly decorative places. Don't hesitate to mix these accent threads on one canvas, as well as stranding different ones together to create new colors and textures. Tapestry, Persian, and knitting yarns can all be used on the same canvas, as long as each is right for the mesh, the stitch, and the ultimate use of the needlepoint.

Always work a sample in the yarns, canvas, and stitches you intend to use before buying in quantity. Canvases and wool sometimes vary from their intended specifications and have to be adjusted. If you have trouble fitting stitches into the canvas, your yarn is too thick and will eventually push the canvas threads out of position. If the canvas shows through your stitches, you may not be using a full enough thread. Before changing yarn or adding an extra strand to your needle, be sure your stitches all lie flat and are not getting twisted, which would make them narrower and thinner.

How Much Yarn You Need

To figure your yarn requirements, calculate the square inches of each color you will need on your canvas. For odd-shaped areas, simply estimate the area generously. Then multiply this figure by the amount of yarn it takes to cover one square inch of canvas in

AMOUNT OF YARN NEEDED FOR NEEDLEPOINT, BY TYPE OF CANVAS AND TYPE OF STITCH

	No. 10 Mono	No. 10 Penelope	No. 12 Mono	No. 5 Penelope
TYPE OF YARN	Persian, full 3 strands; tapestry wool; knitting worsted	Persian, full 3 strands; tapestry wool; knitting worsted	Persian, 2 or 3 strands; tapestry wool; knitting worsted	Persian, 8 strands; tapestry wool, tripled; knitting worsted, tripled; rug yarns
AMOUNT OF YARN*				
Basketweave	36 inches	36 inches	42 inches	18 inches
Continental	36 inches	36 inches	42 inches	20 inches
Half cross	not recommended	28 inches	not recommended	14 inches
Cross	not recommended	66 inches (Persian, 2 strands)	not recommended	24 inches (Persian, 4 strands)
Mosaic	33 inches	33 inches	38 inches	16 inches
Scotch	32 inches	32 inches	36 inches	14 inches
Gobelin	24 inches (Persian, 4 strands)	not recommended	32 inches	not recommended
Brick	26 inches (Persian, 4 strands)	not recommended	28 inches	not recommended
Bargello	24 inches (Persian, 4 strands)	not recommended	24 inches	not recommended
Quick point	. . . .	. . . .	. . . .	18 inches
Turkey tufting, using thumb for loop size	58 inches	60 inches	72 inches	34 inches

*The amount of yarn given is that required to cover one square inch of canvas with the stitch listed using the types of yarn named at the top of the column, except where indicated. A variation of 25% in the amount of yarn needed should be allowed to compensate for loose or tight stitching.

11

any particular stitch. You will find this information on page 11, but if you are using any size canvas or working any stitch not listed, simply work one square inch on a piece of canvas, measuring the amount of wool it takes. Finally, convert this large number of inches of wool needed into yards, which is the way much wool is sold.

For example, you want to make a 13 x 13-inch pillow in basketweave stitch, which requires 36 inches of yarn to cover one square inch of No. 10 mono canvas. You will need to cover 169 square inches of canvas, therefore requiring 6,084 inches of yarn. Converting this back into yards (6,084 divided by 36), you will need 169 yards of yarn. If you are using tapestry wool in 40-yard skeins, buy five skeins (169 divided by 40); if you are using 100-yard skeins, buy two of them; if you are using Persian wool, which has about 44 yards per ounce, buy at least four ounces. (If you are using more or less than the regular three-strand yarn in your needle, adjust your yarn requirement accordingly.) Remember, this is your total wool requirement, which must then be apportioned by colors.

Don't hesitate to rely on the sales people of a needlework shop. Bring your design and specifications to them and they will usually estimate the yarn you need—and, of course, be happy to sell it to you.

NEEDLES

Needlepoint needles, also called tapestry needles, have blunt points and long tapered eyes. They come in sizes 13 through 24, with the lower number needle used on the lower mesh canvas. Sizes 17 and 18 are good, all-purpose needles, and work well on No. 10, No. 12, and No. 14 canvas. Use sizes 19 or 20 needles on No. 16 and No. 18 canvas, and sizes 21 to 24 needles on finer canvases. Size 15 is used on No. 7 canvas and 13 on No. 5 or coarser. Try out different size needles to see which feels best for you.

Keep your needles in a pin cushion, the cork from a wine bottle, or a plastic pill bottle when you are not using them. To keep them clean and deoxidized, run them through a bag of emery, available at notions counters.

PREPARING THE CANVAS

Cut a piece of canvas that is at least five inches wider in each direction than your needlepoint pattern because you will need at least two inches of bare canvas all around for blocking later. To prevent raveling, tape all sides with one-inch-wide masking tape. With the selvage running vertically, mark the top of the canvas. On penelope canvas, the closely paired threads run up and down.

Mark the center point lightly on the canvas. You can find it easily by folding the canvas in half, then in half again. Then center your pattern on the canvas and outline it with a neutral-colored indelible marker, usually adding three extra rows on each side for a "seam allowance."

Having outlined your pattern on the canvas, mark the center of each taped side of the canvas on front and back. These will be your register marks when you later block the piece.

On brown paper, outline the taped canvas—*not* the outline of your pattern but the outline of the entire piece of bound canvas on which you are working— and extend the four register marks on the taped sides to the brown paper (figure 2). Aligning these two sets of register marks will straighten your canvas if it becomes distorted in the stitching. Put this brown paper aside while you work the needlepoint; you won't need it until you are ready to block.

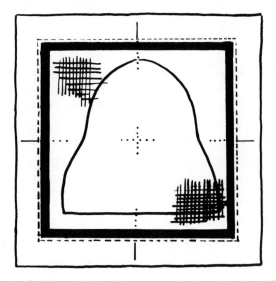

Figure 2.–Outline of bound canvas on brown paper with register marks on the four sides.

If you are upholstering a footstool, dining chair, or anything with an irregular shape, place brown paper on the object and outline it, adding a half-inch seam allowance all around. Or ask an upholsterer to make you a paper pattern.

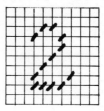

The Stitches

In choosing your stitches, keep in mind not only their appearance, but also the ultimate use of your piece. Stitches with a fairly thick or interlocking backing will wear best and should be chosen for pieces requiring durability. Stitches that are long and cover many threads, particularly on large-mesh canvas, won't wear as well and should be restricted to items like wall hangings. Don't hesitate to experiment with combinations of stitches and, when you have mastered the well-rounded, if limited, repertoire of stitches offered here, consult an encyclopedia of stitches for more advanced work. See page 16 for a sampler showing thirteen different stitches worked on canvas.

CONTINENTAL

BASKETWEAVE

MOSAIC

SCOTCH

REVERSE SCOTCH

CHECKER

GOBELIN

BRICK

FRENCH KNOT

DOUBLE CROSS

DOUBLE LEVIATHAN

TURKEY TUFTING
LOOPED—CUT

If you are left-handed and have trouble making any of the following stitches, turn each diagram in this chapter upside down and try working the stitch by reversing the instructions, substituting right for left, top for bottom. For example, to do the basketweave you would start at the lower left corner of the canvas rather than the upper right.

THE SLANTING STITCHES

The basic stitch used in needlepointing is a slanting stitch that covers one intersection of canvas threads from lower left to upper right. It is worked in any one of three different ways, but from the front it always looks the same.

You can make this slanting stitch by using the continental (sometimes called tent) stitch, the half cross stitch, or the basketweave (diagonal tent) stitch. The main difference among them is the sequence in which the stitches are laid down on the canvas. There are also differences in durability, yarn requirements, and appropriate usage for each stitch that may persuade you to choose one over the other. Read the sections on the three stitches, and try each one out on canvas before making your selection.

The Continental (Tent) Stitch

The continental stitch (figure 3) is the most versatile of the basic slanted stitches and works equally well on both mono and penelope canvas. It provides enough padding on the back to be useful for objects which will see fairly heavy wear. It is excellent for working all kinds of shapes because it is stitched from right to left and from top to bottom, and, by simply turning the canvas upside down, you can change direction. Because of its maneuverability, it is usually used to outline design areas that can be

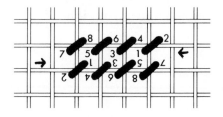

Figure 3.–The Continental (Tent) Stitch.

filled in with another stitch, if desired. The main disadvantage of the continental stitch is that it pulls the canvas out of shape quite severely, although with some effort it can be blocked back to its original dimensions.

Always work the continental stitch from the right side of a row to the left, then turn the canvas around so you come back still working from right to left. Don't pull your stitches too tight; you will get better coverage and less distortion.

The Half Cross Stitch

If you are working on penelope canvas, the basic slanted needlepoint stitch can also be made with the half cross (figure 4). The double threads of penelope are needed to anchor the half cross stitch and prevent it from slipping.

This stitch is always worked from the left side of

a row to the right (even if you are left-handed). To do the return row, turn the canvas around so you will still be stitching from left to right. With the half cross, as with the continental, you must turn the canvas after each row.

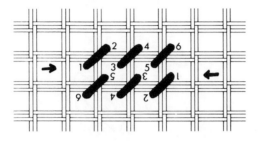

Figure 4.–The Half Cross Stitch.

The half cross stitch requires less yarn, but this yarn saving is made at the expense of having less padding on the back of your piece. Keep this in mind and use this stitch only on objects that will not require much durability. Like the continental stitch, the half cross pulls the canvas out of shape.

A hybrid stitch combines alternating rows of half cross and continental, thus eliminating the constant need to turn the canvas around. After working one row of continental from right to left, return on the next row with half cross from left to right. When worked on larger meshes like No. 5 penelope, this combination stitch is called "quick point."

The Basketweave (Diagonal Tent) Stitch

The third of the look-alike slanted needlepoint stitches is the basketweave, named for the attractive woven pattern it makes on the back of the canvas. It has a number of advantages over the other two stitches, and is probably the favorite stitch of most expert needlepointers. You work the stitch without turning the canvas around after every row. It hardly distorts the canvas, so blocking is a fairly simple

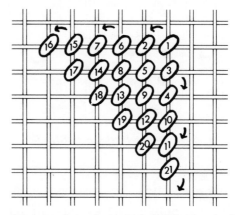

Figure 5.—The Basketweave (Diagonal Tent) Stitch. Sequence of stitches beginning at top right.

process without too much tugging and pulling. And it has the heaviest, most closely woven backing, making it particularly durable and suitable for upholstery, rugs, and other heavy-duty items. Its main disadvantage is the difficulty of maintaining the basketweave sequence in the face of design or color changes. But you can always intersperse continental stitches in areas of basketweave.

Start basketweave at the top right of the canvas and work your rows on the diagonal, going from northwest to southeast (upper left to lower right), then returning from southeast to northwest and back again (figures 5 and 6). Don't be put off by your first look at the diagram; the basketweave is a simple and logical stitch—worked on the diagonal rather

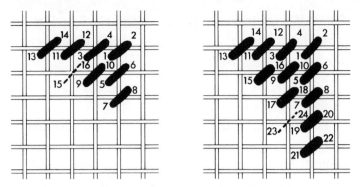

Figure 6.–Left, working basketweave from upper left to lower right; right, returning from lower right to upper left.

than on the horizontal—and just as easy to master as the continental and half cross. Study the diagram with needle, yarn, and a swatch of canvas in hand, and you'll soon see how easily you can master it.

When resuming the basketweave stitch after changing wools or working on another area of the canvas, be sure to continue your rows in the proper direction, otherwise a faint line will show on the

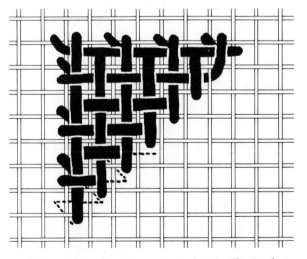

Figure 7.–Working the canvas to maintain the basketweave pattern as it has been established on the back of the piece.

21

front of your piece. If you have trouble figuring out whether you should be working southeast or northwest, consult figure 7.

The Mosaic Stitch

The mosaic stitch (figure 8) is a useful addition to your repertoire. Its boxlike look is an effective background for a centered motif. It has a thick padding on the back of the canvas, so it can be used for articles requiring durability. It works up quickly and, used with alternating colors, it forms a checkerboard pattern for an attractive border. Balanced

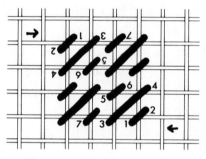

Figure 8.–The Mosaic Stitch.

against these many virtues is the main disadvantage of the mosaic stitch: it tends to pull the canvas out of shape, so don't work it too tightly.

The Scotch Stitch

The Scotch stitch (figure 9) enlarges the pattern of the mosaic stitch. Where the mosaic is worked over two threads horizontally and vertically, the Scotch stitch covers three or even four threads of canvas in each direction. The larger the pattern, however, the more easily the stitch snags, particularly as the canvas mesh increases in size. The stitch does have a

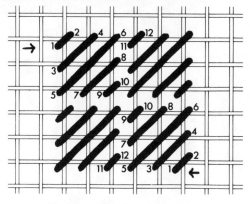

Figure 9.–The Scotch Stitch.

thick backing, which makes it useful for articles where snagging will not be a problem. Keep your yarn flat and untwisted, and work your stitches on the loose side because they tend to distort the canvas.

The virtues of this stitch are many: it covers the canvas rapidly, forms a striking pattern by itself, and combines with other stitches in interesting variations. You can alternate it with squares of continental as in figure 9. Alternate contrasting colors

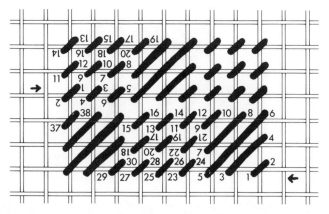

Figure 10.–Scotch stitch alternated with continental stitch, sometimes called the checker stitch.

Figure 11.–The wide checkerboard border worked in Scotch stitch effectively frames a monogrammed pillow.

for a checkerboard border (figure 11). Or reverse the slant of alternate stitches for another interesting effect, as in figure 12.

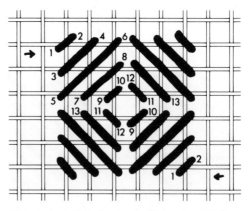

Figure 12.–Reversing the slant of alternate stitches creates another variation of the Scotch stitch.

The cross stitch is a long-time favorite of embroiderers for stitching fabric samplers and decorating table linen. Here it is translated to canvas and worked over one intersection of canvas threads at a time. A variation is stitched over two threads in each direction, making the cross four times as big. The stitch is recommended for penelope mesh only, since it slips on mono and will not form an even row of stitches.

You can make this stitch in two ways (figure 13), either working it individually by crossing each stitch as you make it, or by the "running" method in which you work all the slanting stitches in one direction across the canvas at one time, and return on the same line, crossing those slants to complete the stitch. Either way, be sure the top stitches all slant in the same direction. The running method is much faster than the individual stitch method but does not give

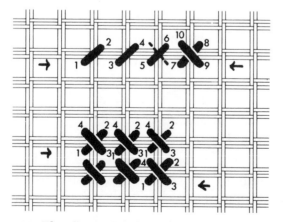

Figure 13.–The Cross Stitch. Worked by the "running" method (top) and by completing each stitch individually (bottom).

you as firm a backing; use it when durability is not a factor and you want to speed along.

You must work the cross stitch in a finer yarn than you are using for other stitches on the same canvas; since the thread intersection is crossed twice (once for each arm of the stitch), a finer yarn will give you the proper weight in the completed stitch. The same amount of yarn is used whether you work the stitch by the individual or the running method.

Choose the cross stitch for outlined areas of your design rather than as a background stitch. It is tedious to do for large areas, but in small spaces it lends interest to a canvas.

THE VERTICAL STITCHES

The Gobelin, brick, and Bargello stitches that follow are all worked up and down over horizontal threads of your canvas rather than crossing intersections as the slanting stitches do. They are recommended for mono rather than penelope canvas for two reasons. One, the yarn covers the canvas better between the single vertical threads of mono than the double vertical threads of penelope. Two, it is easier to count the horizontal threads on mono.

In addition to the attractive patterns formed by this family of upright stitches, there are other advantages. The stitches can be worked in either direction, left to right or the reverse, and up and down in any order. They do not exert a diagonal pull on the canvas and tend to distort far less than the slanting stitches. Because the stitches are worked over more than one thread, they cover ground rapidly and an impatient needlepointer sees a canvas quickly come to life. To cover the canvas adequately, the vertical stitches require thicker yarn (usually an extra strand) than you would use on the same canvas for slanting stitches.

The Gobelin Stitch

Named for the stitch produced on looms at the Gobelin tapestry works in France, the Gobelin stitch (figure 14) also resembles the embroidered satin stitch. Work it over two, three, or four horizontal threads, keeping your yarn flat and untwisted for a neat stitch and good coverage. It makes a quick back-

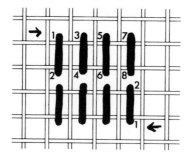

Figure 14.–The Gobelin Stitch.

ground of contrasting texture for a central design done in basketweave or any of the other slanted stitches (figure 15).

The Brick Stitch

The brick stitch is closely related to the Gobelin stitch, but instead of covering the canvas in even rows, the stitches alternate rows in a bricklike

Figure 15.–The Gobelin stitch used as background for a butterfly (page 138) and a frog and lily pad (page 152).

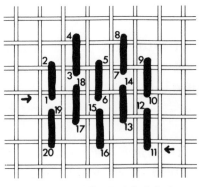

Figure 16.–The Brick Stitch.

pattern. You can work it over two threads, or over four threads for a larger brick pattern, in each case alternating every other stitch.

There are two ways to do the brick stitch (figures 16 and 17) : you can work across the canvas, moving up and down to form the pattern, or you can work across the canvas in the same row, skipping every other stitch and filling in on the return row. Both methods use about the same amount of yarn, but the first gives a thicker backing and the second is a little faster.

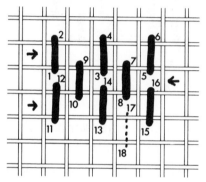

Figure 17.–An alternate method of working the brick stitch skips every other stitch, filling in on the return row.

The advantages of the brick stitch are many. It works up quickly and makes an interesting but unobtrusive background that will not detract from a central motif. It is also attractive in pictorial elements—the roof of a house, for instance.

The Bargello Stitch

Also called Florentine or Flame Stitch, Bargello is really a series of vertical stitches in a particular pattern rather than a single stitch. Whatever the pat-

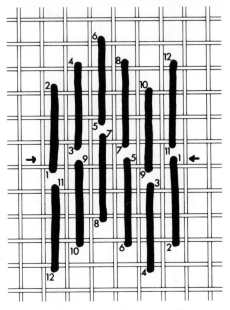

Figure 18.–A basic zigzag Bargello pattern.

tern, the stitch usually covers four horizontal threads of canvas; however, it can also be worked over two, three, four, five, six, and even eight horizontal threads, with the steps between ranging from one to four. See figure 18 for a simple zigzag pattern.

The variations in Bargello patterns are many, all changing with the number of threads the stitch covers, the number of steps up or down, and the points at which these changes are made. The line of stitches can be sharpened, elongated, or rounded, as well as self-enclosed, making possible patterns that resemble hearts, fish scales, scallops, diamonds, hexagons, and so forth. See figures 19 and 20 and pages 124 through 127 for Bargello patterns and how to lay them out on canvas.

Bargello patterns are commonly stitched in a number of graded tones of one or more colors. For ex-

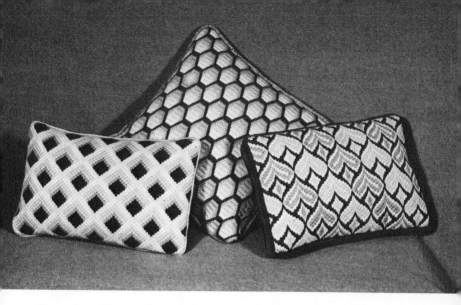

Figure 19.–Three self-contained Bargello patterns similar to the designs on pages 126 and 127.

Figure 20.–Bargello pillows based on the line patterns on pages 124 and 125.

ample, yellows through oranges to red and rust in a rising and falling pattern will give a wonderful feeling of licking flames from which the stitch gets one of its many names.

To work the Bargello stitch, use yarn of appropriate length for your piece—shorter if you only need a small amount, extra long for a continuous line of stitches; the yarn receives less abrasion in a vertical stitch and can, therefore, be used in longer lengths. Be sure to keep your wool flat and untwisted for a neat stitch and good coverage.

SPECIAL STITCHES

Turkey Tufting

Turkey tufting is one of the simplest loop stitches to do and, if cut, makes a tufted pile that can be used

Figure 21.–A shaggy pillow in a plaid design is worked entirely in turkey tufting.

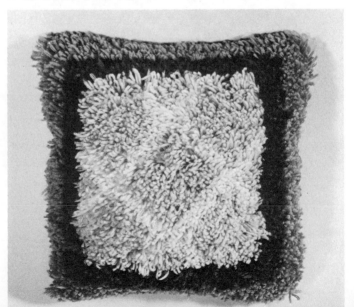

effectively as a rug, a shaggy pillow (figure 21), or a decorative area on a canvas—perhaps as animal fur or shrubbery. It aso makes a lovely fringe. The stitch covers the canvas quickly and won't stretch it out of shape, but it is most extravagant of yarn.

Always work this stitch from the bottom of the canvas to the top, and from the left to the right (figure 22). Any change will entangle you in already formed loops. From the front of the canvas, put your needle down through one mesh, holding a tail of yarn as long as you want the pile to be (one-half to one inch works well). Bring your needle up in the same horizontal row but one mesh to the left, then insert the needle two meshes to the right into that same row and come up in the original starting mesh, pulling the yarn tight. To form the second stitch, with your thumb hold down a loop of yarn as long as the tail

Figure 22.–Turkey Tufting. Upper left and right shows how to form one stitch. Lower diagram shows sequence of stitches worked from bottom to top and left to right.

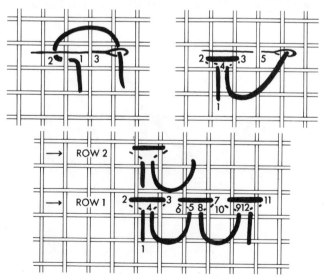

on the first stitch. Proceed to the next stitch in the same manner, always holding the loop with your thumb until the stitch has been completed and pulled tight. When you come to the end of the row, cut the yarn and begin the next row of stitches on the left again, working in every other horizontal row. Each stitch will take two vertical threads and, because you skip every other horizontal row, two horizontal rows as well. Thus, if you are using No. 10 canvas, you will be making five stitches to the running inch and five rows of stitches to the inch, or twenty-five stitches per square inch.

To cut down on yarn waste, use the longest lengths you can handle.

French Knot

Use the decorative French knot stitch alone or in clusters to create berries, eyes, jewelry, and other special effects. You can form the knot on bare canvas, working from one mesh to an adjoining one, or

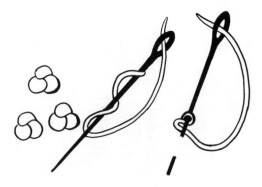

Figure 23.–The French Knot.

you can embroider knots right over existing needlepoint.

To make the stitch (figure 23), bring your needle
out at the required position. Hold the yarn down with
your other thumb and wind the yarn twice around
the needle. Still holding the yarn firmly, insert the
needle in the mesh adjoining the starting point. Pull
the needle and yarn to the back and secure it for a
single French knot.

The Double (Smyrna) Cross Stitch

The double cross stitch (figure 24) is worked over
two horizontal and two vertical threads of canvas,
and combines a vertical cross with a diagonal one.
The only trick is to be sure that, when making
more than one stitch, all the top strokes cross in the

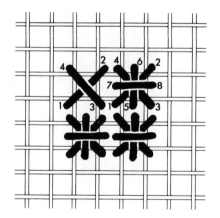

Figure 24.–The Double (Smyrna) Cross Stitch.

same direction. Use this bumpy stitch when you
want a more pronounced or larger effect than you
can get with a French knot.

For larger and higher bulky stitches, use the Double Leviathan (actually a quadruple cross), which is worked over four threads in each direction (figure 25).

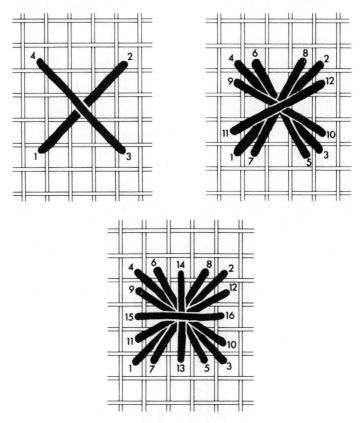

Figure 25.–The Double Leviathan Stitch.

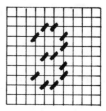

Finding Your Design

It's great fun to work on a pattern that is uniquely your own, and the point of this book is to allow you to do so—easily and inexpensively.

Once you have discovered how simple it is to combine elements from Chapter 11—Patterns and Components—into a needlepoint composition, you may then want to become even more adventurous. You may want to fill a certain spot in your home with a particular motif, color, or shape. You may have a special interest or be attracted to one period in decoration. Some of these ideas can be worked out with design components from this book; others will spring from a variety of sources.

Here are some possibilities to spark your own ideas:

Add to Your Collection

Whether you collect shells or Staffordshire figures, dolls or Doughty birds, your collection can be the focus for a needlepoint design. Most small items make an effective overall pattern, or a treasured object can become the central motif of a canvas. You can also borrow the colors from one collection—Delft, for instance—or reproduce shapes from another, such as primitive musical instruments.

Family Comes First

Some of the most attractive pieces of needlepoint record treasured details of happy family life (figure 26): a trip, the family pet, an award, a vacation house, all the events that inspire the nostalgic question, "remember the time. . . ."

Or turn your youngster's best drawing into a needlepoint picture. Children's artwork is often effective in needlepoint because it is flat and simple. If your children are not artistic, transform their favorite character from a book or a bedtime story into a needlepoint design.

The Animal Kingdom

Since it is easier to copy a drawing of an animal than a photograph, collect sketches of your favorite beasts in magazines or books—and refer to Chapter 11. Or you might choose the primitive quality of a

Figure 26.–A colonial house, important dates, and hobbies are noted in this sampler recording the life of one family.

Figure 27.–Lively giraffes and a fierce leopard inspire pillows that are sure to please an animal lover.

jungle painting by Henri Rousseau or a "Peaceable Kingdom" by David Hicks. If you are doing a group of animal pillows (figure 27), consider an overall pattern of skin markings (see pages 136 and 137).

How Does Your Garden Grow?

If you have a patch of daffodils, why not stitch a matching bouquet? Lilacs, roses, zinnias, geraniums, any favorites from your garden more than double their appeal when reflected in needlepoint (figure 28). Copy the flowers from seed packets, catalogs, or other botanical prints if you don't find them in Chapter 11.

Figure 28.–Stylized daisies, bluebells, and anemones are massed on a footstool for a gardener.

Figure 29.–Paintings by Paul Klee, left, and Vasili Kandinski, right, are translated into needlepoint.

Your Favorite Painter

Many artists, particularly modern ones, translate effectively and easily into needlepoint. Matisse, Mondrian, Klee, and Kandinsky, for example, can often be copied intact (figure 29). You may also want to borrow only one element of a picture or simplify the composition. Look through art books in your library, auction catalogs, or visit museums.

A Message in the Medium

Needlepoint a word, a phrase, or lines of poetry, using a small mesh, or penelope that can be split. A much-visited hostess in Hawaii displays a pillow reading, "You *are* leaving by Sunday, aren't you?" A well-known needlepoint shop offers this maxim:

Figure 30.—A black hand and a white hand holding a dove symbolize brotherhood and peace on this pillow.

"You can't be too rich or too thin." Stitch a symbol (figure 30), a political slogan, or even a single word like LOVE or EAT.

Look for the Unexpected

Good ideas for needlepoint designs are all around you, sometimes where you would least expect them. Children's book illustrations are especially good because they are decorative and simplified (figure 31). Record album covers, travel posters, or wrapping paper might yield a pattern. One young woman even covered a bedroom chair with the Pucci print she traced from her slip. Ethnic sources also offer inspiration: a Navaho rug, Polish and Hungarian embroidery, Swedish wall hangings.

Highlight your wallpaper, slipcovers, draperies, or hooked rugs by using them as design sources for a needlepoint pillow or other accessory, or pick up the colors or design of your fine china in dining chair covers. You can copy an entire pattern exactly, or feature a single element. Or adopt just a color scheme in a Bargello pattern.

Decorate to a Period

In addition to specific designs from your draperies or rugs, many pattern ideas suggest themselves from the general period of your decor. Any good book on interior design can supply you with ideas, as can interior decorators. Here is a random list to which you can easily add:

Figure 31.—Two book covers capturing the ingenuous simplicity of children's art make an effective pair of pillows.

Figure 32.–A Bargello seat cushion ties with tassels to an Early American child's chair.

AMERICANA (figure 32): Patchwork; Pennsylvania Dutch hex signs, hearts or tulips; quilt patterns, eagles. Colors: Indigo blues, brick reds.

SPANISH-MEXICAN: Desert and tropical flowers. Colors: hot pink, orange, red; black scrolls against white.

EIGHTEENTH CENTURY ENGLISH: Chinese porcelain and other oriental motifs, Imari ware, shells, bamboo, scrolls, china patterns (figure 33). Colors: rich red shades of Chippendale to soft greens, blues of Hepplewhite and Sheraton.

FRENCH PROVINCIAL: Toile de Jouy prints, sunburst, checked ginghams. Colors: rust reds, bronze golds, faded blue.

EMPIRE: Laurel wreath, Napoleonic bee, lyre, Egyptian influences. Colors: gold and black.

VICTORIAN: Cabbage roses, fruit, mixed flowers. Colors: black background for red, green, and gold.

Figure 33.–A flower-bedecked circular pillow based on a museum piece of eighteenth century Lowestoft china.

ART NOUVEAU: Tiffany glass patterns, peacock feathers, Beardsley prints. Colors: stained-glass colors, black and white, mauve.

POP/PSYCHEDELIC: Andy Warhol soup can; Peter Max posters, heart-shaped American flag. Colors: Day-glo brights, black, white.

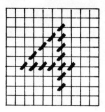

Design, Composition, and Color

When you complete your first original design on canvas, you have a happy surprise in store. No matter how slight your talent, when the stitches are all in, the final result of an artistic venture in needlepoint always seems to have a more finished and satisfyingly professional look than expected.

As added insurance for success—especially if it is your first attempt to plan your own pattern—here are some random hints to keep in mind as you work with design, composition, and color. They apply whether you are drawing freehand from your own imagination or whether you are putting elements together from other sources, from Chapter 11 of this book, for instance.

DESIGN

■ Simplify the lines. An elaborate design is more difficult and less successful on canvas; an uncluttered pattern will be more striking and dramatic.

■ Use broad, fluid lines where possible in place of tight, close ones. Remember that your drawing must ultimately be worked out in squares on the canvas, therefore straight lines or boxlike shapes will be easiest. Large curves can be handled better than small ones. Avoid small circles in a design because there is no way to round off a circle that must be made in four stitches—you'll have a square every time.

■ Aim for a flat, decorative effect, especially in your early designs when you are learning the possibilities and limitations of the medium. As you advance in expertise, you may want to add shading and intricate perspective.

■ If you are planning a design that is perfectly symmetrical, remember that, although the sides will have a general similarity, they will look a little different due to the slanting nature of the basic stitch. You can make them perfectly symmetrical, however, if you use the Gobelin stitch.

▪ To design an integrated composition, make sure the individual elements have some relationship to each other. Seemingly unrelated elements may be used in one composition if the group does, in fact, have some meaning to either the stitcher or the recipient—that being the unifying theme—but ordinarily, disparate components undermine an integrated design.

▪ When assembling design elements, keep the composition simple. Needlepoint stitches themselves add diversity to a canvas. Discipline yourself to leave out elements, not put more in. A novice's most frequent mistake is to let the canvas become too busy.

▪ Background space is an important part of a strong and effective composition. Don't crowd your design components unless that is the effect you want.

▪ To compose a design of many elements, trace each one on separate scraps of tracing paper. Then move them around on a piece of paper marked with the outline of your finished object to find the positions where they combine most attractively. This way you can experiment with a design before committing yourself on canvas.

▪ Traditional concerns of any artist—focal point and balance—apply particularly to needlepoint in this way:

Focal Point

The focal point stands out from the canvas because of color, size, or other feature. It is the center of interest and draws the eye in its direction. A focal point gives your design a sense of unity. When you plan, color, or design details, remember to let one element dominate. It may be a vivid splash of color against a subdued background, for instance, or a round shape against straight lines. A focal point is not, as a rule, exactly centered.

Balance

Balance is a general art rather than an exact science. You would not, for example, put all the heavy elements of a design on one half of the canvas, but you might balance two small components against one bulkier one. The upper half of a design should not look heavier than the lower half, unless it is done for special effect. In an all-over design, don't use a single accent; instead use three, perhaps in an asymmetrical position. In the end, your main concern is eye appeal; your composition is balanced if it doesn't look oddly askew or tilted.

COLOR

- If you are completely confused as to your color direction, lean on the traditional guidance of a color wheel (figure 34). For a complementary color scheme select colors that are opposite each other on the

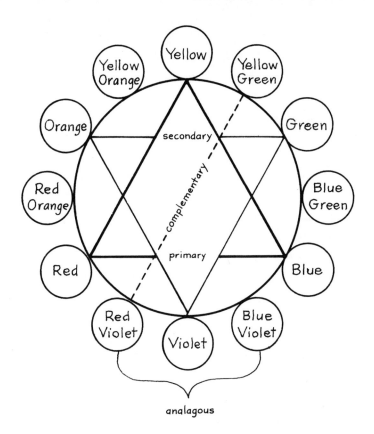

Figure 34.–Color wheel showing primary, secondary, complementary and analogous color schemes.

wheel, as, for example, blue and orange. Or pick an analogous color scheme with any two colors directly next to each other, as blue and blue-green. These simple fundamentals will safely guide you to a harmonious color scheme; expand each basic color, if you like, with a range of tones.

▪ For a sharply contemporary design, you might choose clashing, dissonant colors instead of harmonious colors. With these, judgment and a trained eye are the only guides.

■ A monochromatic—single hue—color scheme carried out in a number of shades from dark to light gives an unexpectedly rich appearance, especially in Bargello patterns.

■ Unless you are planning an all-over pattern—perhaps butterflies or flowers—that calls for a multiplicity of gay hues, limit yourself in the beginning to two or at most three colors, using them in different shades if you want more variety. It's tempting for a novice to use too many colors that will look muddled in the end.

■ Choose your background color to contrast sufficiently with all parts of the design which touch it, either darker or lighter.

■ Black and white sharpen and point up all other colors. Use black with lighter shades, white to set off darker colors.

■ Bright and light colors look a shade darker when worked.

■ Try your colors out in the hand before buying them. Most shops encourage you to group yarns to see which colors work well together.

■ If the exact color you are looking for isn't available, combine strands from two or three of the closest shades into one three-stranded yarn (for No. 10 canvas). This mix will be close to the exact color you want, and will give an interesting tweedy look as well.

■ To enliven a simple color scheme, add one jolt of strong color—a scarlet lady bug, for instance, against a background of green leaves.

■ For simple shading, use tones of the same color, stitching the lightest shade closest to the source of light and the darkest shade farthest away from the source of light.

■ For more subtle shading, combine two or three shades of the same color into one three-stranded yarn. Again, using a mix of lighter shades, work away from the source of light on your canvas, substituting darker strands as you go.

■ If you want your needlepoint to bring warmth to a room, choose a color scheme with yellows, reds, browns, and orange tones; for cool notes, blues and greens should predominate.

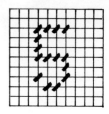

Putting Your Design on Canvas

Once you have chosen your design, there is no great difficulty in putting it on canvas. This is the step that seems insurmountable to many people, but if you follow the simple guidelines in this chapter, you'll discover how easily you can do it yourself. This is the process for which you pay dearly at needlepoint shops.

There are various methods of putting your design on canvas; your choice will depend on where you have found a pattern and your own inclination.

If your design is the right size for your canvas, needs no enlarging or reducing, and is already on a single sheet of paper with no writing or printing on the back, you can simply trace your design right onto the canvas. Designs from wallpaper, fabric, posters, and drawings are all transferable in this manner. Proceed as follows:

1. Position the design face up under the canvas, and tape it in place with masking tape.

2. Lay design-and-canvas on a glass table or on a piece of glass resting on two supports. Put a lamp on the floor to light the canvas from underneath. If you don't have a glass-top table, tape the canvas to a large window pane where the sun can shine through.

3. Trace the design, which will now show clearly through the canvas, using an indelible marking pen in a light or neutral color, or in the colors of the finished needlepoint. Don't use a black marking pen if your yarns are light-colored; the dark lines will show through.

NOTE: Use only completely indelible markers—the Studio Magic Marker, the AD marker, or India ink —available in art supply stores and in a variety of colors. It's always prudent to test your marker on canvas by washing with soap and water and steaming with an iron to be certain it is indelible.

TRACING PAPER METHOD

Your design may be the right size without enlarging or reducing and yet not be suitable for direct tracing on canvas. This is true, for instance, if you take a design from a book or magazine with printing on the reverse side of the page, or from a dinner plate that is too opaque to let light through. In these instances, simply add the intermediary step of copying the design on tracing paper. Then follow the method of transfer to canvas described above.

ENLARGING OR REDUCING YOUR DESIGN

If the design you want to needlepoint is not the right size for your canvas, there are various ways to enlarge or reduce it.

1. The simplest method of changing the size of any design is by photostat. Simply take your design, or a tracing of it, to a photo enlarger for photostatting. He can enlarge or reduce your design to any size, crop it to change its proportions, and even isolate one element in a picture for enlarging or reducing. Ask for the positive image (the negative you customarily get has white lines on black background and is harder to work with). Some firms photostat up to 54 inches by 170 inches—called jumbo stats—and others can piece together any number of photostats to get the size you want. Look these companies up under Photo Copying in the classified pages.

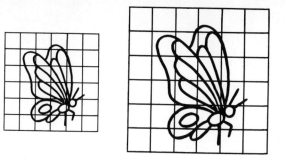

Figure 35.–The "square" method of enlarging a design.

2. You can also change the size of your design by the "square" method (figure 35). Mark your design, or a tracing of it, into squares: one-quarter-inch squares for a small design, half-inch or one-inch squares for larger designs. On another sheet of paper the size you want for the finished needle-point, mark off a similar set of squares; in this case, however, while the *number* of squares will be the same, the *size* of the squares themselves will not be. Make them smaller if the design is to be reduced, and bigger if the design is to be enlarged. For example, if your original design is marked in 24 half-inch squares and you want to double its size for your finished piece, rule the second paper into twenty-four similarly placed squares of one inch each. If you want to reduce your original design by half, simply mark your second paper into twenty-four similarly placed quarter-inch squares.

To transfer your design, copy the drawing square by square from the original paper to the enlarged or reduced squares. You will get a reasonable reproduction, but not as accurate as a photostat.

Once you have a drawing or photostat of your design in the proper size for transfer to canvas, follow the directions for putting your design on canvas described under *Direct Tracing*.

SKETCHING ON CANVAS

It is risky to sketch directly on the canvas without trying your design out on paper first. But if you have enough talent for it, work lightly with a pencil, correcting your drawing by erasing until you are satisfied with it. Then go over the drawing in India ink or indelible markers and erase all other pencil marks; they will smudge your wool. If you plan to work with light-colored yarns, paint over pencil erasures with white acrylic paint or the erasures will show through. As you can see, it is far safer to sketch your design on paper and, when it is finished, transfer it to canvas by the direct tracing method.

PAINTING YOUR CANVAS

Once your design is outlined on canvas, there are a variety of ways to indicate color:

1. Crayon, paint, or simply write the colors on your paper design, then use it as a guide when you needlepoint.
2. Draw colored lines through the areas of the canvas in the shades of yarn you have chosen.
3. Color solid areas of canvas with indelible markers, available in a variety of shades.

4. Outline areas of color in indelible markers if your design is bold and simple.
5. Paint the complete design in color on your canvas. This will look like the painted canvases sold in needlepoint shops.

If you feel comfortable with paints, don't hesitate to try painting on canvas. You will find there are distinct advantages to having a painted canvas; you will always have your color guide with you (without having to refer to your design paper), and if your wool doesn't quite cover the canvas in a few places, the underlying paint of the same color will keep the white canvas threads from showing through.

The best paints to use are acrylics, which come in bottles or tubes in a variety of colors and are easy to handle. They are water soluble before they dry, making clean-up easy; they can be thinned with water for lighter or darker shading; and, while quick-drying, they stay liquid long enough to give you time to work. Once the acrylic paints dry (a matter of hours under normal circumstances), they are absolutely permanent and impervious to water, solvent, and dry cleaning fluid. You can use them without fear that they will later run and spoil your finished canvas. Oil paints can also be used with safety, but they are messier to work with and take much longer to dry.

Here are some tips for working with acrylic paints:

■ Add enough water so that paint flows easily and sits on top of canvas, but not so much that the paint soaks through. Ideally, very little paint should show through on the back. You want your paint thin enough to flow easily and not so thick as to clog the meshes.

- Work with a fairly dry brush to avoid saturating the canvas; it will lose its sizing and stretch if it gets too wet.

- Use a fine brush for the outlines, a wider brush for covering large areas of canvas.

- Paint over mistakes after they have dried with white acrylic paint (if you are using white canvas).

WORKING FROM GRAPHS

Working from a graph is the adventurous process of starting out with a blank canvas and stitching the design with a paper graph as your guide. One advantage to having a design on graph paper is that you can experiment with placement of stitches on paper in pencil, rather than on canvas with needle. It is essential to use graph paper for accuracy in portraying geometric shapes like circles or mirror images, and for letters, numbers, or legends of any kind. It is particularly useful for repeat patterns as well. Work out all figures carefully on graph paper before stitching on canvas.

As a rule, you work from designs already graphed, but it is possible to draw or trace a design onto graph paper yourself.

Here are some tips for using graphed designs:

■ If your graph is not already divided by heavy lines, in addition to the smaller squares, draw these darker lines every inch on both graph paper and on canvas. (On No. 10 mesh, these lines will fall every tenth thread.) In this way, you will have close reference lines from which to count and locate your stitches.

■ If you are following an entire pattern on graph paper, be sure to mark the exact center of the graph paper and also the exact center of the canvas so you can count out accurately. The center of the canvas is easily found by folding the canvas in half once and then in half again.

■ If you are working a geometric pattern or one that relies in any way on exact number of stitches—in a border, for example—be sure to work it out carefully on graph paper first. Then count the threads on canvas rather than measuring the canvas with a ruler because canvas sometimes varies imperceptibly, but enough over a long span to throw off your calculations. For instance, if you have worked out a Greek key border on graph paper that requires 100 stitches along each side, count those 100 stitches on each side of the canvas rather than measuring ten inches (if you are using No. 10 canvas).

■ In general, you will outline each area of color on the canvas in continental stitch, filling in later with basketweave.

For detailed instructions on how to work the graphed patterns and components in Chapter 11, see pages 65 to 69.

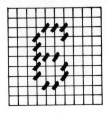

Needle Notes

Now that you've chosen your design and you've got it on canvas, let's take a look at some of the many tricks of the trade that will make needlepoint easier as well as more professional looking. Some are obvious and you would find them on your own; others take long experience to discover. Here are some tips that can give you answers before you come to the questions. They apply in general, no matter what size canvas or yarn you are using, or what kind of project you have in mind.

- Don't work with yarn that is longer than 18 to 24 inches; longer strands may start to fray after being pulled through the canvas mesh too many times. Knitting worsted in particular is weakened by this abrasive motion.

- To thread your needle, never lick the yarn as you might cotton sewing thread; you will get a mouthful of fluff and be no nearer your goal. Instead, try one of these two methods:

1. Pinch the end of the yarn tightly and insert it into the eye of the needle, in much the same way as you thread a sewing needle with cotton thread.

2. Fold the yarn over the pointed end of the needle, pinching the yarn tightly against it. Then withdraw the needle, insert the doubled yarn into the eye of your needle, and pull through.

- To start stitching on a blank section of canvas, put your needle through one hole from back to front, leaving about one inch of yarn hanging in the back. Hold this tail with your fingers so the first five or six stitches will catch it, anchoring it in place.

An alternate method of starting on a blank section of canvas is to knot the end of your yarn and insert your needle from front to back of the canvas about an inch away from and in the path of your starting stitch, leaving the knot on the face of the canvas. Your subsequent stitches will eventually anchor the tail; simply cut off the knot when you work up to it and continue stitching.

■ To start a fresh length of yarn next to a section of already worked canvas, run your needle through four or five stitches in the back and come up at the proper point to begin.

STITCHING TIPS

■ Work at an even tension, pulling the yarn tight enough to avoid any slack but not so tight as to stretch the canvas out of shape or to leave bare canvas threads showing. If you're not sure of the proper tension, work on the loose rather than the tight side. A looser stitch covers the canvas far better than a tight one and can always be adjusted later; a tight stitch is harder to repair.

■ When the yarn becomes twisted, hold your piece of canvas upside down and let the needle and yarn fall free and unwind themselves.

■ When yarn is worked down to its last two or three inches, weave it in back through finished stitches to secure it. If you can, work it into the line of stitches just completed. This is practical for two reasons. First, you can remove and repair one or more stitches by taking out one length of yarn, leaving the neighboring work on either side undisturbed. Second, yarns of darker color sometimes show through as a shadow on the front if they are anchored on the back through white or lighter color yarns.

■ Clip the tag ends of all finished yarns often so they don't get entangled as you work along.

▪ However you work the basic needlepoint stitch—in continental, half cross, or basketweave—the slant of the stitch must always be from lower left to upper right (that is, running between southwest and northeast). If they go in the opposite direction, your canvas will look "left-handed." And if some slant in one direction, some in the other, you will have a problem where they meet—unless, of course, you are doing it for some special effect, like ruffled fur on an animal.

▪ For additional interest, you may want to mix stitches: contrast patterned stitches against plain ones, textured next to smooth, small areas of pattern set off by larger areas of plain stitches.

▪ When working a multi-hued canvas, save time by keeping at hand a needle threaded with each color of yarn.

▪ If you use a thimble to sew, try it for needlepointing. Your fingers often need extra protection as they push the needle through the canvas.

WORKING THE CANVAS

▪ If you are working on a piece of canvas that is too large to be held flat in your hand, roll up the sides of the canvas, leaving an open field where you are working. You can pin the rolled canvas with extra tapestry needles or safety pins, taking care to secure them through the meshes without splitting the threads.

▪ Keep work clean by storing it in a plastic bag.

▪ Work central designs before doing the background, stitching the most complicated and shaded areas first. This prevents "bunching" of threads in the middle of the canvas, which sometimes happens if background stitches crowd the unworked center meshes.

■ When ready for the background, start at the upper right corner of the canvas if you are doing basketweave or continental, the upper left if you are using the half cross. For solid color backgrounds, don't work separate small areas at a time; you will end up with faint shadows and ridges on the front of the piece where these separate areas meet.

■ If your design has lines of dark stitches—for instance, letters, numbers, or an outline—on a light background, stitch the background first so the light yarn doesn't pick up fuzz from the darker yarn. You can mark the location of the lettering or lines with lightweight cotton thread. After finishing the background, stitch right over the cotton thread with your needlepoint yarn; there is no need to remove the thread if it is fine enough.

■ When you are finished working one block of color, you can carry your yarn to another area by weaving it through the back of the intervening stitches. If there are no worked areas to anchor into, simply carry the yarn across the bare canvas and start your next section; the yarn will eventually be anchored when the intervening area is stitched.

■ Because continental and basketweave are worked from right to left and from top to bottom, or diagonally in those directions, it is sometimes hard to get to a section of the canvas that is to the right or above where you are working. In that case, simply turn the entire canvas upside down so that the top becomes the bottom, and you will find that the formerly inaccessible areas are now conveniently to the left or below where you are working. When changing the direction of your needlepointing, be sure to turn the canvas around the full 180° and not just 90°.

■ When splitting penelope canvas to do detailed work, spread the threads evenly apart with your needle. Basketweave is a particularly good holding stitch on the resulting smaller gauge mono canvas since the threads tend to fall back into the double-mesh penelope pattern. To keep the basketweave stitches even, repeatedly spread the canvas with your needle for three or four squares around each stitch as you work.

■ After you have finished stitching areas of your canvas—particularly light-colored ones—you can baste a piece of clear plastic over the area to keep it from getting soiled. Plastic dry cleaner bags are handy and useful.

■ Because of the nature of canvas, the circular, fluid, or oval shapes of your design will have to be fitted into the gridlike limitations of the canvas mesh. This is not difficult. A curve becomes a series of steps, a circle becomes a cluster of squares. Just be sure that the shape is large enough, or the canvas mesh small enough, to allow for gradual rounded-looking lines on the square grids.

To translate curves onto canvas squares, simply stitch over the intersection that is closest to the line of the design. Sometimes your stitch will be outside the drawn line, sometimes inside, but you will find that when the stitching is completed, the eye will compensate for the seemingly jagged steps of a

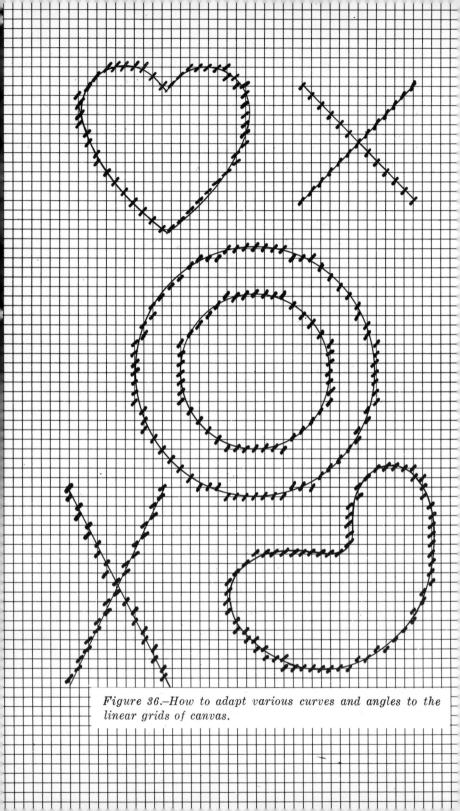

Figure 36.—How to adapt various curves and angles to the linear grids of canvas.

smooth line. Figure 36 illustrates how various shapes are translated onto canvas.

FINISHING OPERATIONS

■ Work two or three extra rows of stitches—preferably basketweave—around all sides of your finished piece to make a "seam allowance" for sewing a pillow or other item and for framing a needlepoint picture (the extra stitches will be hidden under the lip of the frame)

■ Into the back of every finished piece of needlepoint weave two or three strands of every color yarn you have used. These should undergo the same cleaning and blocking as the piece itself so they will exactly match the needlepoint, should you ever need to make repairs on worn or torn stitches.

■ If you have worked a curved or diagonal shape, don't trim the canvas until after the piece has been blocked and is ready for mounting or finishing. The rectangular or square piece of canvas on which you did your stitching will keep its shape best.

REPAIRS

■ To pull out stitches in order to correct mistakes, snip with a pair of small, sharp scissors, taking care not to cut the canvas threads. After you have gotten the first stitch or two cut, pull out succeeding stitches with the eye end of the needle until you have dislodged the entire thread. (If you have finished the thread in the back of its own stitches, you won't be disturbing any neighboring threads.) If you do not want to eliminate the entire thread but only a stitch or two, cut those stitches and pull out two or three inches on either side of the mistake until you have enough to thread the needle and weave into the backing to secure.

■ To take out stitches you have just worked, never reinsert the needle back through canvas. You are almost certain to split existing stitches in the back and become badly entangled. Instead, unthread the needle and pull the stitches out one by one with the eye end of the needle. In fact, as you pull the stitches out one by one, you may find that you have stitched through some wool in the back. You will have to split the yarn carefully as you undo these stitches, then retwist it. If you are badly enmeshed in split yarn, you may very well have to take out and replace the entire length of yarn.

■ Never re-use pulled-out yarn.

■ If stitches are pulled so tightly that canvas shows through, or you didn't use the proper thickness of yarn in the first place, go over those stitches with one or more strands of same color yarn. The additional strands will fill in the canvas and blend with the original stitch.

■ To repair ripped, torn, or weak canvas, simply cut a piece of matching canvas a little larger than the disaster area. Baste in place with cotton thread, taking care to match the repair piece mesh for mesh with the original canvas. Stitch over the double thickness as you would if it were only the original single thickness of canvas.

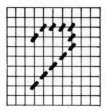

What to Make of It — and How

The range of objects enhanced by needlepoint is enormous. Here are a few ideas to which you can add your own:

pillows	hassocks
belts	golf club covers
headbands	pockets
chokers	vests
eyeglass cases	cummerbunds
wall hangings	golf tee holders
framed pictures	chair seats
luggage rack straps	stool cushions
coasters	bridge table covers

*Figure 37.–Family portraits are grouped becomingly in a
pair of different, but related, needlepoint frames.*

typewriter covers
slippers
rugs
fireplace screens
wastebaskets
handbags or evening
    bags
pin cushions
director's chair covers
stadium blanket covers
tote bags
box covers

stair risers
kneelers
bricks for doorstops or
    book ends
covers for all books,
    including Bibles,
    photo albums,
    memo pads,
    appointment books,
    telephone books,
    check books, and
    cookbooks

For most of these items, you can make your own pattern, then stitch and mount the needlepoint yourself as with the picture frames in figure 37. In general, you simply measure what you want to cover, leaving seam allowances when necessary, then outline those measurements first on brown paper (for later blocking) and then on canvas (figure 38). If you are making luggage rack straps, a typewriter cover, or a set of covers for a director's chair, you may have the original to use as a guide. And home sewing companies sell patterns for belts, suspenders (figure 39), vests, headbands, and other items of clothing.

Figure 38.–A shield-shaped cushion is outlined on canvas. Owl (page 156) and leaves (page 141) are already worked.

Unless you are unusually handy, leave furniture, handbags, and large rugs to be mounted by a professional, as well as any objects to be bound in leather, such as slippers, book covers, and wallets.

Figure 39.–A pair of suspenders uses one of this book's border designs (page 134) edged in a contrasting color.

PILLOWS

Pillows can be made in all sizes, from mini rectangles of 8 by 5 inches to large "sit-upons" twenty-four inches square. A pillow thirteen or fourteen inches square is a good size, especially in No. 10

canvas; it accommodates a nice variety of designs, and is well scaled for most furniture (figure 40).

A knife-edge pillow is easier to make than a box pillow, and is usually edged with welting or fringe, or finished with corner tassels. To make various edgings, see pages 94 to 97.

Figure 40.–A detail from a Peruvian tapestry, two Matisse designs, and an Albers abstract form a needlepoint art gallery.

To make the pillow, place blocked needlepoint right side up on a table and lay the welting around the sides with the finished edge of the welting facing the center and the unfinished edge pointing out toward the bare edges of the canvas (figure 41). Baste and then sew along the outside rim of the welting, making sure that on all four sides of the

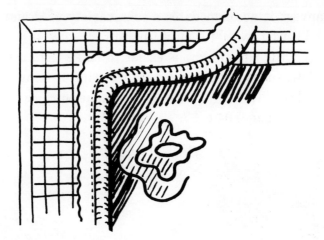

Figure 41.–Welting is attached to the right side of finished needlepoint with the raw edge facing out.

pillow your seam is inside at least two rows of needlepoint (worked needlepoint holds a seam far better than bare canvas does).

Now lay the backing material face down on the needlepoint and welting, right sides together, and sew along your seam line, turning all four corners but sewing only three sides. Leave the fourth side open. Trim backing material and canvas to within one inch of the seam and closer at the corners. Add a thin line of glue inside the cut edges to prevent unraveling and turn the pillow inside out.

If your pillow is a standard size, you can insert a ready-made dacron or kapok pillow, available at variety and department stores. If it has an irregular shape, you will have to make an inner pillow out of muslin and stuff it with layered dacron or down purchased from an upholsterer. Slip stitch the fourth side.

If you are not welting your pillow, follow the same

directions, simply joining the backing directly to the canvas, right sides together. Pillows are usually backed with felt, velvet, corduroy, linen, even suede; welting is made from the backing material or cotton welting can be purchased ready-to-use at notions and sewing counters.

For a box cushion (figure 42), cut a strip of backing material long enough to go around all four sides and as wide as you choose. Follow instructions for knife-edge pillow, making two seams to form the box rather than the single seam for the knife edge. Insert a readymade box cushion if you can find the right

Figure 42.–Box cushions can be square or rectangular as in this welted seat for a piano bench.

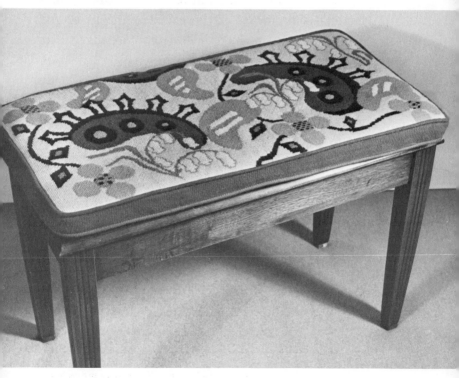

size, or cut a piece of foam rubber to exact size. Blind stitch backing to bottom of pillow.

Instead of fabric sides, you can needlepoint the four sides on the same canvas you worked for the top of the cushion. Cut them apart, leaving one inch all around, and join them into one continuous strip following the instructions on page 91.

EYEGLASS CASE

Work your canvas to measure 3 by 6 inches. Cut a piece of felt 6 by 6½-inches and join the two 6½-inch sides together flatly with a laced, zigzag stitch (figure 43). Double the felt and center this seam so that on each side of it there is 1½ inches of felt. Seam one end one-half inch from the edge. Trim excess felt and turn inside out.

Trim excess canvas to within one inch on all sides of the blocked needlepoint and to within one-half inch at the corners. Fold under and whip excess canvas to underside of needlepoint. Blind stitch your needlepoint to the felt, covering the side with the center seam (figure 44).

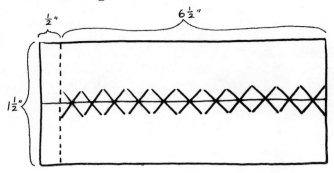

Figure 43.–Eyeglass case before needlepoint is mounted.

Figure 44.–An eyeglass case combines a snail (page 139) and lilies-of-the-valley and leaves (page 142).

BRICKS

Bricks to be covered are about 8 by 2¾ by 3¾ inches, but measure yours before you begin. Make your needlepoint brick jacket two rows larger in all dimensions. To finish, first upholster the brick in muslin or felt, gluing the material to the brick or use the self-adhesive felt backing that is sold by the piece in hardware or notions stores. Then slipcover the brick by sewing four corner seams on the needle-point, right sides together; trim the excess canvas from the sewn seams to within an inch all around and one-half inch at the corners. Turn the four sides under at the bottom, and, with heavy thread, lace

Figure 45.–A Bargello pattern (page 125) mounted on a brick, and a paisley pattern (page 136) ready for finishing.

opposite sides of the needlepoint jacket together. Sew or glue a piece of felt on the bottom to cover the lacing. See figure 45.

BOOK COVERS

The simplest books to cover are those whose contents slip in and out and are not bound or glued to the inside of the spine of the book. You will find an

inexpensive assortment of them in variety stores—
bridge tallies, photo albums, address books, and so
forth (figure 46).

Make your pattern two rows larger in all dimensions than the book to be covered. After stitching
and blocking, cut the raw canvas edges to one inch
on all sides and one-half inch at the corners. Then
glue the raw canvas to the inside of the covers, miter-

*Figure 46.–A memo pad cover and a pencil holder utilize
the bee and ladybug (page 138) and the daisy and leaf (page
144).*

Figure 47.–"Icarus," a paper collage by Henri Matisse, is mounted in a ready-to-assemble metal frame.

ing the corners (see page 93). To finish, glue felt or heavy decorative paper to the inside of both covers.

PICTURES IN NEEDLEPOINT

Trim the excess canvas from your blocked needle-point, leaving one-and-one-half inches all around and one-half inch at the corners. Retape the sides of the raw canvas. Lay this trimmed canvas face down under a backing board cut one stitch smaller than the needlepoint. If you want a soft look to your needlepoint painting, insert a layer of foam rubber or layered dacron between the backing board and the canvas. Fold back the half-inch seam allowance at the four corners, and then fold back the sides, stitching them together with heavy thread to make mitered corners (see page 93). Across the back, lace opposite sides of the canvas together with carpet thread, then secure to the backing with strips of Mystic tape. Cover the lacing with a piece of brown paper to keep dust out.

You can hang the mounted needlepoint without a frame by gluing a picture hanger on the back, or by sewing a decorative curtain ring to the top of the needlepoint. You can also frame it in one of the ready-to-assemble metal frames now sold at most art supply stores (figure 47), or bring it to an art store for custom framing.

If you are framing a sampler, tape a diagram of all the stitches used on the back of the mounting.

WALL HANGING

Wall hangings (figure 48) are customarily lined and hung without a backing board, often on a curtain rod. Line them according to instructions on page 94. Hardware is usually available at needlepoint shops.

Figure 48.–Sixteen different stitches are worked up into a Mondrian-type wall hanging.

BELT

Trim excess canvas to one inch on all sides and one-half inch at corners, then turn under and tack the bare canvas to the underside of the needlepoint. Back with velvet or suede and blind stitch to the needlepoint. If the belt is exactly waist size or smaller, you can stitch leather thongs to the backing for tying; if the belt is larger than waist size, fasten with large hooks and eyes or use a buckle (figure 49).

Trim excess canvas to within half an inch of the worked canvas, turn under, then carefully whip it to the back of the needlepoint. Blind stitch a length of ribbon wide enough to cover the band in back and long enough for tying at the back of the neck. Or close with Velcro.

Figure 49.–Traditional patchwork becomes a contemporary belt with the addition of a huge, shiny buckle.

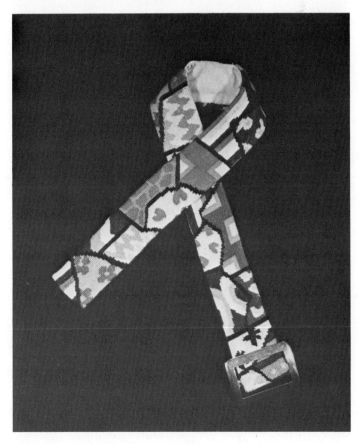

Figure 50.–A desk set uses fur (page 137), a giraffe (page 161), birds (page 157), a shrub (page 158), and letters (page 139).

PENCIL HOLDER OR WASTEBASKET

Any tubular container—a frozen juice can, for instance—can be finished into a pencil holder (figure 50). The same technique applies to covering a wastebasket. Measure the height of the container and subtract one inch, then the circumference, adding half an inch. Work your needlepoint to these dimensions. After blocking, seam the needlepoint, right sides together, to fit the circumference and press seam flat. Trim the excess canvas to the height of the container, and slip over the cylinder. Line the inside with felt and glue a wide ribbon around the top and bottom of the container to hide the bare canvas edges.

The simplest way to cover a box is to upholster it first in fabric. Stitch the needlepoint exactly to size, then blind stitch in place. Your needlepoint can cover an entire box top (figure 51) or be centered on an attractive fabric like velvet. Trim the edges of the needlepoint or the fabric with decorative braid, ribbon, or gimp, if desired.

Figure 51.–A lily-of-the-valley (page 142), a snail (page 154), and two abstract flowers (page 145) cover the top of a box.

Although a large rug should be handled by an expert, you can finish a small rug yourself. Needlepoint it to exact dimensions—no seam allowance—and then turn under the raw canvas edges and whip them to the back of the worked area. Line the rug according to instructions on page 94. Use either a nonskid material for the lining, or stitch strips of it to the under edges of the rug. You might want to fringe the rug with long turkey tufting (see page 32).

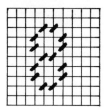

Finishing Touches

When you are through working your canvas, you will want to finish it with as much care as you stitched it. This will usually mean blocking to restore it to its proper shape; it may also involve connecting sections or adding such finishing touches as fringes and tassels.

BLOCKING

On a clean wooden board—plywood works well— tape or tack the brown paper on which you have already marked the outline of the canvas and the four register marks (see *Preparing the Canvas*, Chapter 1). Lay the needlepoint face down on the brown paper. Dampen the back of the needlepoint by steaming with an iron held well above the actual surface of the canvas; if you don't have a steam iron, sponge the back of the canvas until it is wet but not saturated. Secure the four corners with nonrusting pins or tacks through the bare canvas about one inch away from the worked needlepoint (never tack through completed needlepoint). Then, pulling on opposite sides of the canvas to keep the tension even, tack all four sides at one-inch intervals, stretching until the canvas conforms to its pattern on the brown paper and the register marks on the bound edges of the canvas meet those on the brown paper pattern (figure 52). Leave the needlepoint face down on the board until dry, perhaps two days. A badly misshapen canvas may have to be blocked two or three times.

Figure 52.–To block needlepoint, tack piece down at one inch intervals; be sure that register marks on paper and canvas meet.

90

Blocking flattens the stitches somewhat. If you want to fluff them up, steam the face of the worked canvas, holding the iron a few inches above—but not touching—the surface of the canvas.

After blocking it, it is good practice to machine stitch a row of stitches around the worked portion of the canvas, as close as possible to the needlepoint. This prevents unraveling in the event that you cut the bound edges in mounting the canvas.

JOINING SECTIONS OF CANVAS

There are three ways to join canvas pieces that have been worked in sections:

1. Seam the canvas exactly as you would two pieces of fabric, right sides together (figure 53). Then press the seam open. This is the simplest method and works well if you don't have to match meshes or a pattern.

2. Hem each section to finished size *plus* one thread on the edges of the canvas to be joined. Then match

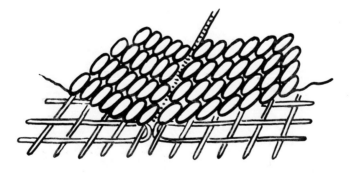

Figure 53.–Joining two canvases by the seaming method.

the edges mesh for mesh and join the two sections of canvas together by working one row of continental stitch in an appropriate color yarn (figure 54).

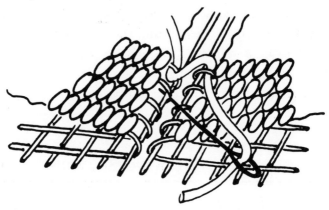

Figure 54.—Joining two sections of canvas by matching edges and whipping them together with a row of continental stitch.

3. Lap the last three or more rows of one section over the first three or more rows of the next section, carefully matching the bare meshes. Secure by whipping the overlapping sections together with heavy thread, covering only one intersection at a

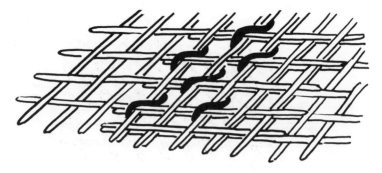

Figure 55.—Joining canvas pieces together by overlapping them, then stitching through the two thicknesses.

time so thread won't show through (figure 55). Then stitch the design or a border over the double thickness in basketweave, continental, Gobelin, or cross stitch. A faint ridge will show. Only join canvas of the same mesh and weight.

MITERED CORNERS

Many different objects require a mitered corner when finishing, among them wall hangings and pictures, belts, chokers, book covers, and any article

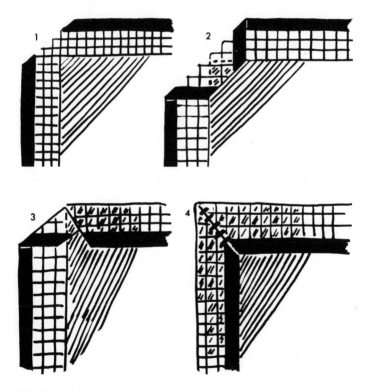

Figure 56.–Four steps in mitering a corner: trimming the bare canvas, turning it under, folding adjoining edges, and securing the finished miter.

that should lie flat. First trim the bare canvas on all four sides to within one inch; then diagonally trim each corner to within a half-inch of the corner point and run a line of glue inside all cut edges. To miter the corner, turn under the diagonal edge and fold each adjoining edge over it, as in figure 56. Whip the abutting canvas edges together and press flat.

LINING NEEDLEPOINT

Whenever lining a piece of needlepoint, whether for wall hanging, bell pull, belt, choker, cummerbund, or other object, use firmly woven material.

After your piece has been blocked, trim the excess raw canvas to a half-inch all around, cutting away any extra bulk at the corners and running a line of glue inside the cut edges to prevent unraveling. Baste, then hem, the raw canvas edges to the back of the needlepoint, taking care that the stitches do not show through to the front.

With the needlepoint face down, measure a piece of lining a half-inch larger all around than the hemmed needlepoint. With the right side of the lining facing up (the wrong side of the lining will be next to the wrong side of the needlepoint), turn the lining under three-quarters of an inch and sew with a slip stitch.

EDGINGS

Most pillows are improved with cording, fringe, or tassels, as are some wall hangings and upholstered pieces. Commercial cording and fringe, purchased at notions counters and sewing centers, work very well if you can find the right color.

Cording or Welting

Lay the welting on the face of the blocked needlepoint with the finished edge of the welting facing center and the raw edge pointing out toward the bare edges of the canvas (figure 41). To finish pillow, follow directions on page 76.

Fringe

Use commercial fringe in exactly the same way as the welting, keeping the cut ends of the fringe facing in toward the center of the pillow when you sew it to the needlepoint.

To hand fringe a pillow, needlepoint your canvas exactly to size, then in the next row on all four sides work one row of turkey tufting to form the fringe, turning the canvas as you go (figure 22). Outside of the row of fringe, work two rows of needlepoint in one of the three basic stitches (half cross, continental, or basketweave). You will sew between these two rows when mounting the pillow. If the fringe gets in your way as you try to work these two rows, or when you are joining the canvas to the pillow backing, tape the fringe temporarily to the needlepoint with masking tape. To mount a pillow, follow the directions on page 76.

Tassels

Make your tassels from needlepoint yarn, if possible, picking up the background color, one or more of

95

the dominant shades, or even a potpourri of all the hues in the canvas. Then follow these steps (figure 57):

1. Cut two nine-inch lengths of yarn and set aside.
2. Wind yarn for tassel loosely around the long end of a playing card twenty times for a thin tassel, thirty times for a medium thick tassel, and forty times for a heavy tassel. If making a multicolored tassel, simply divide the total amount of yarn needed by colors.
3. Using one of the lengths of yarn you set aside, tie the tops (A in figure 57) of the wound yarn tightly, keeping the end of the tie separate from the rest of the tassel.

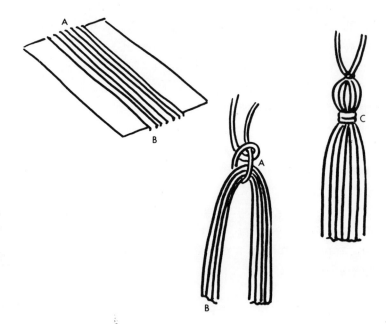

Figure 57.–Three steps in making a tassel: winding the yarn, cutting the bottom, and tying the "head."

4. Cut the wound yarn at the bottom (B in figure 57) of the playing card.
5. Using the second length of yarn you set aside, tie a knot around the body of the tassel about one inch below the top (C in figure 57) and let the ends of this tie hang down and mingle with the rest of the tassel.
6. Trim the yarn ends to an even length.
7. Sew the top tie (A) into the pillow corners close to the head of the tassel when making the pillow.

FINISHING TIPS

- If you are not ready to finish a blocked piece of needlepoint right away, store it so the stitches won't get crushed or out of shape: lay it flat in a drawer if it's small enough; roll it around a cardboard tube and cover with tissue paper; or hang it from the cross bar of a wire hanger by safety pins and cover with a dry cleaner's plastic bag.
- Clean and freshen needlepoint with a cleaning fluid, or send out for dry cleaning.
- Protect your needlepoint against soiling with a fabric protector like Scotchguard. Mist it on carefully so it sits on top of the stitches without soaking the needlepoint.
- To glue needlepoint to cardboard, wood, or other porous material, use a white glue like Elmer's Glue-All or Amco White Glue. They dry colorless, hold well, and won't damage the needlepoint.
- Whenever you cut the canvas to within a half-inch of the needlepoint, also run a thin line of glue

inside the cut edge. This is a second line of defense against potential unraveling to reinforce the row of machine stitching you have sewn.

■ Needlepoint combines well with many other fabrics, so finish your work with backings of velvet, crushed velvet, cotton, felt, suede, corduroy, or linen.

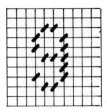

A Gift That Is Part of the Giver

If it's true that the best gift is to give of yourself, needlepoint makes the perfect present. Rows of stitches speak eloquently of your feelings when the recipient considers the time—that priceless commodity—that you have put into making a gift.

The occasions for bestowing needlepoint are endless: weddings, housewarmings, christenings, weekend visits, not to mention the more obvious birthday, Christmas, Mother's Day, Father's Day. Nor is there an age limit when it comes to those delighted to receive needlepoint. A bright wall hanging would please an infant in his crib, while a perfectly shaped neck cushion could delight an octogenarian. Even a teen-

Figure 58.–Monogrammed letters (page 128) centered on a field of abstract flowers (page 145) cover a bridge tally.

age boy might graciously accept a pillow or typewriter cover recording his current major interest. Look at the list in Chapter 7 for a wealth of ideas.

When planning a needlepoint gift, make it as personal as you can. Everyone likes to see his name in print, so try to include the potential owner's initials (figure 58). In fact, a monogram or an initial can itself become the design. Center a giant initial or monogram on a plain background, and frame it with a border such as the Scotch stitched checkerboard pattern pictured on page 24. The initials of the recipient can also form a border around a central motif.

For other personal designs, use a zodiac sign or symbol (figure 59). Or give a family crest to someone with pride in ancestry. (Check your local library for reference books picturing many family crests.) Commemorate the Alma Mater by stitching the college emblem (figure 60).

Figure 59.–Leo the Lion (page 168) stitched on a pillow is an appropriate gift for anyone born between July 23 and August 22.

You can also focus on a special interest, using any of the components and designs in Chapter 11:

For a Bird Watcher

Memorialize a frequently spotted warbler on an all-weather, vinyl backed pillow for more comfortable bird watching, or on the cover of a binocular case.

Figure 60.–A Princeton pillow and a Tufts seal ready for mounting will strengthen old school ties.

For a Gourmet Cook

Almost all fruits and vegetables make attractive patterns. For instance, stitch a bundle of asparagus and a single artichoke to cover two bricks to keep cookbooks together, or cover the top of a recipe book with fruits or vegetables (figure 61).

For a Sportsman

Catch a mallard duck in flight for a hunter; stitch a team insignia on a stadium blanket cover for a football fan; decorate a tennis racquet cover; put an official baseball or basketball on a pillow for a teenage boy (figure 62) or facsimiles of swimming or riding ribbons for a young girl.

For a Gardener

Flowers are always in season for needlepointers (figure 63). Cover the canvas liberally with a profusion of flowers, or stitch one perfect bloom. Consider dividing your canvas into quarters for the seasons: an oak tree with pale green buds of spring, full green leaves of summer, fall's flamboyant coloring, and finally, snow-laden bare branches.

Figure 61.–The lemon slice (page 150) doubles as a lime in green yarn. Title is from the alphabet on page 131.

Figure 62.–A basketball framed in a checkerboard pattern which has been needlepointed in Scotch stitch.

For a Weekend Host

Focus on a special activity of the weekend. A scarlet lobster could bring back the fun of a clambake. Long walks with the family dog might be recalled in a needlepoint portrait (figure 64). If a map of the area hangs in your host's house, make a tracing of it and work it up later in needlepoint.

Figure 63.—A tiger lily (page 140), a pansy (page 143), and a huge daisy (page 144) make a bouquet of coasters.

Figure 64.—A portrait of a canine friend backed by a patch-work sampler worked in forty-three different stitches.

Figure 65.–A honeymoon trip through England, France, Switzerland, and Italy is recalled in needlepoint.

For Your Favorite Author or Book Lover

Stitch a needlepoint representation of his favorite book jacket; if you use No. 10 penelope, you'll be able to include the title and author's name in petit point by separating the canvas into No. 20 mesh count.

Many sentiments are appropriate for a wedding or engagement gift—bride's and groom's initials, with or without love knots; church steeple, wedding ring; doves—worked as a ring pillow to be framed later, or as the cover for their wedding album. You might catch the bride's bouquet in needlepoint and frame, or copy a map of their honeymoon trip (figure 65).

Figure 66.–Ancestral roots go back for three generations in this needlepointed family tree.

107

For a Christening

Give a baby a needlepoint picture of the family tree (figure 66) or copy an old Pennsylvania Dutch birth record and include the newborn's name. For a girl, an old-fashioned needlepoint doll becomes a stuffed treasure. A small nursery rug with favorite toys or fairy tale characters is a handsome gift, although the time involved may limit it to first grandchildren.

For a Housewarming

Make a small needlepoint picture of the new house, then frame it as table top art or to hang on the wall. Or copy a flowering shrub from the garden of a house whose planting is its pride.

For the Needlepoint Enthusiast

Stitch a carry-all tote bag for her own needlework, or prepare and paint a pattern on canvas so she can have the fun of making it herself.

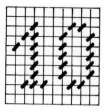

Needlepoint as a Family Affair

Most mothers harbor the fond hope of discovering a hobby they can companionably share with their children. Partly, it is self-interest; any pastime is more fun if done in company. Partly, it is an honest desire to equip a child with as many creative accomplishments as possible. And partly, it is the practical and endless search for something to do on rainy days or on long car trips. Needlepoint is an eminently satisfactory solution for both parent and child. For a youngster, it's exactly what mother is doing, not a watered-down version of an adult pastime. From mother's viewpoint, there is absolutely no way for even the messiest child to spill, stain, or track canvas and yarn across the kitchen floor.

By the ages of six or seven, children are usually capable of working a simple canvas if the mesh is large enough; needlepoint, after all, is only an extension of the cardboard sewing cards which are a staple in every kindergarten. Teenagers often enthusiastically adopt needlepoint as a means of self-expression; they can follow any of the directions given in other chapters of this book.

You can plan a single family project with everyone stitching on different segments of a rug or large sampler, or you can start your children on separate unrelated canvases of their own. Whatever their early projects are, here are a few points to keep in mind:

■ Begin with a coarse canvas like No. 5 penelope. It is easy for children to work with the large squares, and they will be pleased with their quick progress. By the time youngsters are eleven or twelve, they will have the patience to work on a small project on No. 10 mono.

■ Use yarn remnants from your own supply. You will be surprised to see how far the scraps from your past canvases will go.

■ Plan the final use of the project with your child. It's more fun to make a pillow, a pin cushion, or a picture than to work without a goal.

■ Children from six to eight can probably handle the continental or quick point stitches most easily. The Gobelin is another easy stitch for young children. By the age of ten or twelve, many children will prefer the challenge and fun of the basketweave stitch. There is no reason, of course, why a child shouldn't attempt any of the stitches in this book. Refer to

Chapter 2—The Stitches—let your child study the diagrams and watch you do the stitches slowly, then try them himself under your supervision.

■ If your child's interest flags, lend an unobtrusive hand with seemingly endless backgrounds or complicated parts of the design. Typically, children begin a needlepoint project with enthusiasm and then get bogged down in the middle; a wise mother will help out over the rough spots.

■ Keep your child's design as simple as possible. Some artistic children want to design their own canvases; while this is feasible, they are likely to draw something too small or detailed for easy needlepointing. Many of the designs in Chapter 11 can be worked by children.

THREE DESIGNS FOR YOUNG CHILDREN

The Eye-of-God

This is a simple design, which a child can complete without help (figure 67). Draw a four-inch square on No. 10 mono canvas, then start a child with the continental stitch at the lower right corner of the square. After the bottom line has been stitched from right to left, the child turns the canvas to continue stitching around the square, until he ends up in the center. He should use short lengths of yarn and change colors each time the needle is rethreaded. The multicolored effect supplies design interest.

While this isn't proper needlepoint technique (all continental stitches should slant in the same direc-

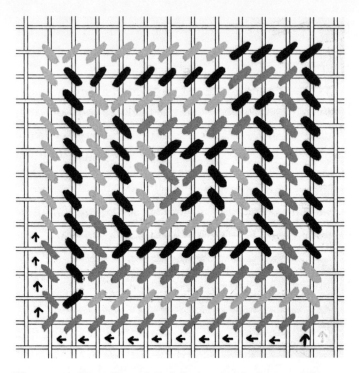

Figure 67.–Start Eye-of-God design in the lower right corner, follow arrows, turning canvas, until center is reached.

tion), it is a good way to introduce a young child to needle and canvas. It encourages freedom to experiment with color, and it results in a charming facsimile of the Eye-of-God talisman of the Peruvian Indians.

A Chess and Checkerboard

On No. 5 penelope canvas, mark a pattern of seven-stitch blocks, eight to a row. If you are using No. 10 mono, mark each side into fifteen-stitch blocks. In either case, you will have a canvas divided into sixty-four blocks, making a checkerboard about twelve inches square. Work each block alternately in red and black, using the continental or basketweave stitch. Needlepoint three rows of black stitches around the outside edges for a border. To finish, block and then turn under excess canvas and baste to underside. Cut a piece of felt the size of the gameboard and attach to bottom with fabric mounting glue, or use the green felt self-adhesive table protectors that are sold in notions counters and hardware stores. For a sturdier gameboard, you can even mount the felt-backed piece to cork or plywood. Alternately, you can frame it and hang it on the wall when not in use.

School Pillow

Block letters are easy and interesting to do. Young children will enjoy stitching their school initials in school colors for a pillow of their own. Using the block alphabet on page 131 as a prototype, work out your child's school initials on graph paper, enlarging them to proper size for the pillow you are planning. Center the design on the pillow, marking the initials in indelible marker. Follow the instructions on page 76 for finishing a pillow.

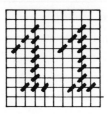

Patterns and Components

You don't need artistic talent or any drawing ability to use the designs in this chapter. They were planned to serve as the raw material for your own creativity. On every page there are multiple components or elements. You can use each one alone as a central motif, multiplied for a repeat pattern, reversed, flipped, turned around, or tilted to any angle. They are designed to work in combination with each other. Let your imagination be your guide. Try your hand at something like the bouquet in figure 68. You can place a tiger in a garden of flowers as we did on the cover, or create something as wild and decorative as suggested by figure 69. In the footstool in figure 70

Figure 68.–A spring-time bouquet arranged from a group of the garden components on pages 139 through 145.

Figure 69.–A border (page 133) frames two sides of this design which incorporates abstract flowers (page 145) on a background which can be marble, wood, or fur (page 137).

115

as well as in the vest in figure 71, you can see how more of the elements combine with each other.

Almost all of the elements or components are drawn on a ten-to-the-inch grid, with each inch marked by a heavier line.

In some of the animal designs, the grid has been reduced to ten-to-three-quarters-of-the-inch. This enables you to make a larger animal than could be drawn on the page. That is, a tiger which measures 7½ inches on the page will automatically translate into a ten-inch animal on your canvas if you simply follow the grid. To combine them in the same scale

Figure 70.–The butterfly (page 138) on this stool is set off in an interesting manner by its rope border (page 134).

Figure 71.–A vest incorporates a zodiac sign (page 165), animal heads (page 163) and a garden fantasia (pages 139-145).

with any of the other components, count out the grids on your canvas by the method described below. (Of course, if you want the animals the size they appear in the book, you can trace them directly from the page, ignoring the grids.)

Once you have decided which elements you want to stitch, there are two ways to use the actual designs: by tracing or by gridding. (If you want to enlarge or reduce a design, follow any of the methods described in Chapter 5.)

TRACING

To combine components, first trace them on pieces of tracing paper to compose your design. Then mark the outline of your finished object on a large piece of tracing paper and try out various elements in different positions within the outline. If you want a bouquet of roses, for example, trace the flower and the bud, then copy them on your paper as many times as you wish, turning or reversing them to form a bouquet; do the same for the leaves.

When putting elements together, don't be afraid to place one in front of or behind another. For example, in the book cover pictured on page 86, the giraffe's legs are partly hidden by a shrub. On your tracing, simply erase the obscured part of any component before transferring the design to canvas.

When tracing on paper or on canvas, you are not actually using the grids. They will be helpful, however, when you start to stitch because they give a rough guide to the number of stitches within the component.

GRIDDING

You should use the gridding method when you are stitching any of the designs on the reduced grids if you want them larger than they appear on the page. You may also use the gridding method to transfer any of the other components to canvas or to combine them, although it is easier to make a tracing. Here are detailed instructions, which apply to any of the patterns in this chapter, for using the grid method.

1. Locate the area on the canvas where the design will go. If you want to stitch the owl on page 156, mark with an indelible marker in a neutral color the heavy intersection where one of the eyes will fall. Extend these two lines vertically and horizontally

until they cover the dimensions of the bird. Then draw parallel lines on your canvas every ten vertical threads and every ten horizontal threads (if you are using No. 10 mono, this will be every inch). You have now duplicated the book's heavy grid on your canvas and are ready to translate the bird design into stitched needlepoint.

2. Outline each area of color with the continental stitch, and later fill it in with basketweave, if possible. Small areas may be more easily filled with continental. Remember that with each intersection of the grid you will be deciding where to put that stitch, because many stitches will fall between exact intersections. If you need help, turn to page 68 to see how different shapes are translated into the rigid squares of canvas.

3. When you have stitched the bird on canvas, you will probably have the ends of grid marks showing on the bare canvas. Ignore them; they will be covered when you work the background.

You can combine any of the elements in this chapter by following the grid method; that is, by duplicating the grid overlaying the design on the page onto the actual canvas. If you wish to combine two or more elements whose heavy grids don't coincide, simply mark the canvas in separate areas for each of the components. Figure 72 shows three components combined into one composition, even though the three sets of heavy grids on canvas, if extended across the entire composition, would not join up together.

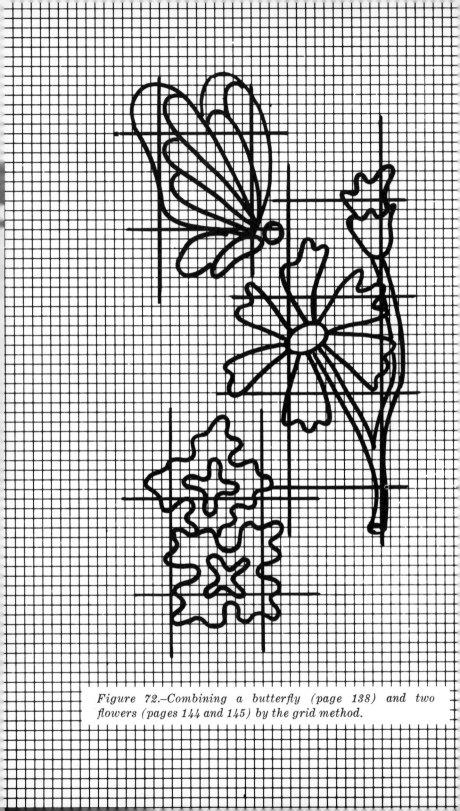

Figure 72.–Combining a butterfly (page 138) and two flowers (pages 144 and 145) by the grid method.

■ When stitching any of these design components, don't worry about the precise line; it may not fall exactly on a canvas intersection. The designs can be varied or modified in any way to suit your taste and the limitations of the canvas; indeed, flexibility will make any design even more your own.

■ Shading and color are indicated by three tones of gray plus black and white. They are intended only as a guide; you can, of course, follow them exactly, that is, use the same color every place black or white or the same shade of gray appears, or you can use any color any time a color change is indicated.

■ Whenever you use a border, plan it entirely on graph paper before starting and use the grid method to transfer it to canvas. Don't rely on laying out any border by ruler directly on canvas; canvas measurements are sometimes inaccurate. This also applies to numbers and letters or monograms.

■ In addition to the borders on page 132, 133, and 134, you can design your own border by repeating any small element in this chapter—for instance, the tulip on page 135.

■ Use the overall patterns on pages 136 and 137 with imagination. For example, the lower one on page 137 in rust and white would be giraffe markings; in shades of green it would resemble alligator skin. Depending on the colors, the other design on the same page could be zebra or tiger markings, striations of wood or marble, or even a psychedelic abstract.

■ These same overall designs on pages 136 and 137 can be made to cover areas of any size without enlarg-

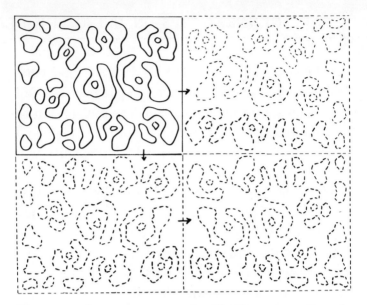

Figure 73.–Cover more ground with the same pattern by flipping it over and down according to the arrows.

ing their patterns; simply flip them up, down and to each side as many times as necessary (figure 73).

BARGELLO PATTERNS

While all other designs in this book are recommended for No. 10 canvas, the Bargello patterns are suggested for No. 12 mono. (For a smaller pattern they can also be worked on No. 16 mono, using 2 strands of Persian yarn instead of the 3 strands used on No. 12.)

Start by centering your pattern on the canvas in both directions. You can find the center stitch by folding your canvas in half, and then in half again. Locate the center of your pattern and make that center stitch on the canvas. You can work Bargello

Figure 74.–A Bargello sampler showing at top and bottom, two line patterns (pages 124 and 125); at left, Byzantine turrets (page 126); and, at right, from the top, scallops, boxes, and hexagons (page 127).

patterns in all directions, from right to left, left to right, and up and down. On the hexagon, scallop, turret, and box, work one whole section as a guide to follow. On the flame stitch or the wave—both continuous line patterns—work one "tracking" row completely across the canvas as your guide for subsequent lines of color. Figure 74 is a Bargello sampler showing the six patterns which follow.

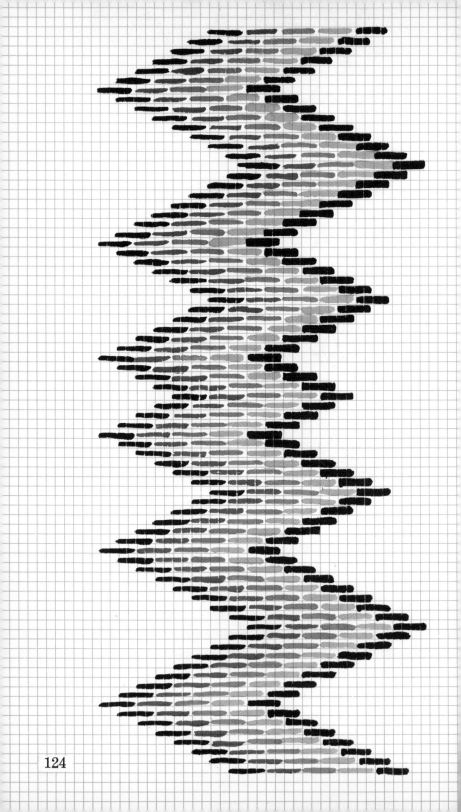

124

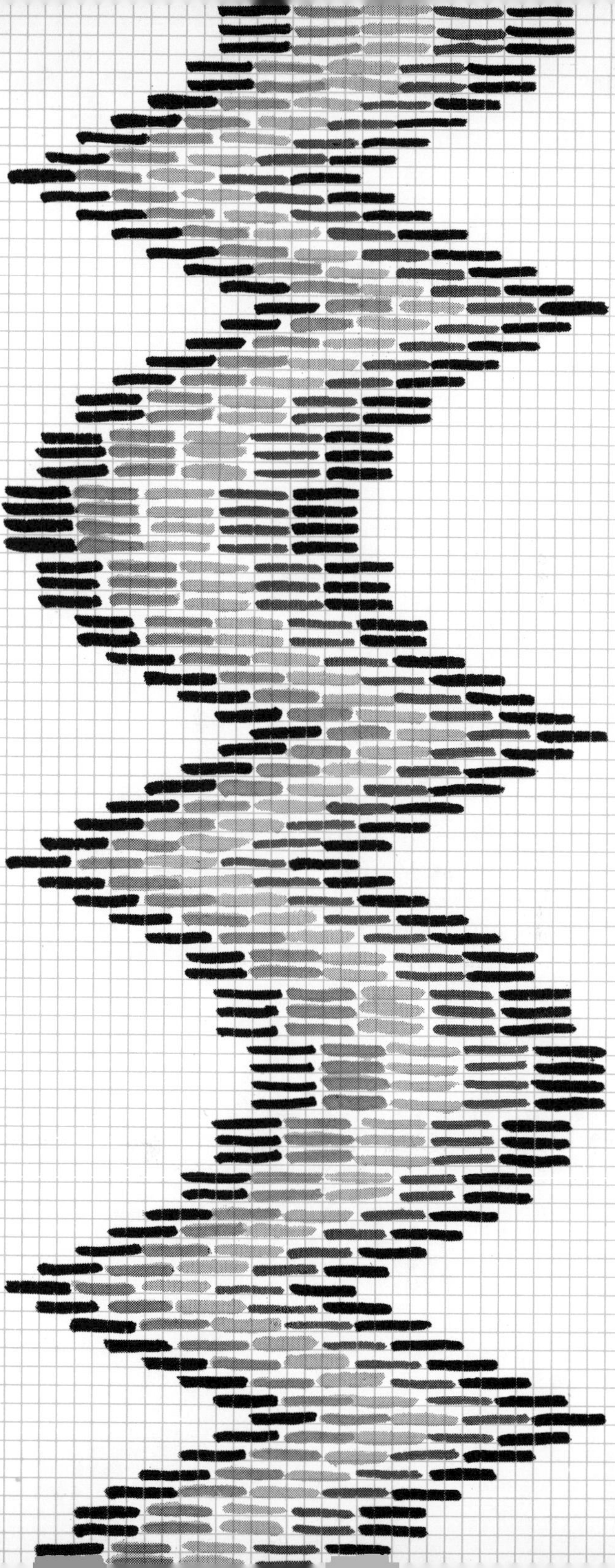

126

127

128

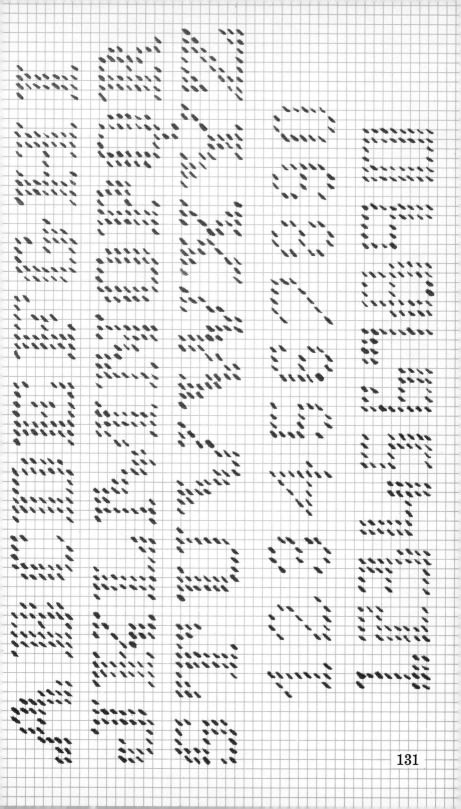

132

133

134

135

136

137

138

140

142

143

144

145

146

147

151

153

155

157

160

161

162

163

ARIES   March 21 to April 20

TAURUS   April 21 to May 20

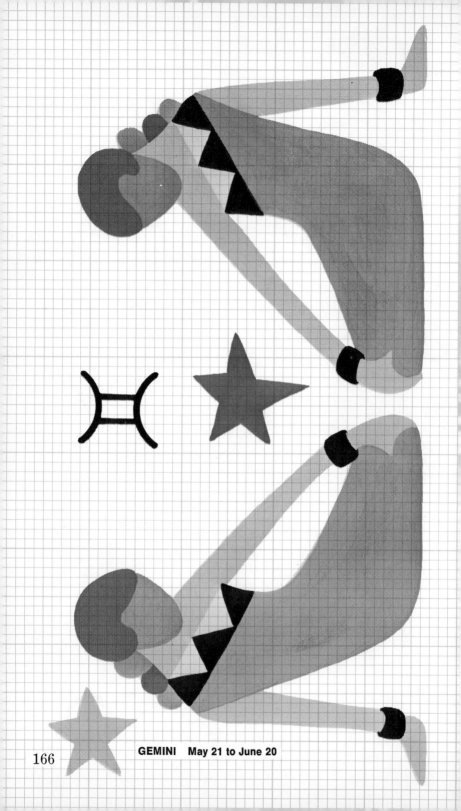

166   **GEMINI   May 21 to June 20**

CANCER   June 21 to July 22

LEO   July 23 to August 22

VIRGO   August 23 to September 23

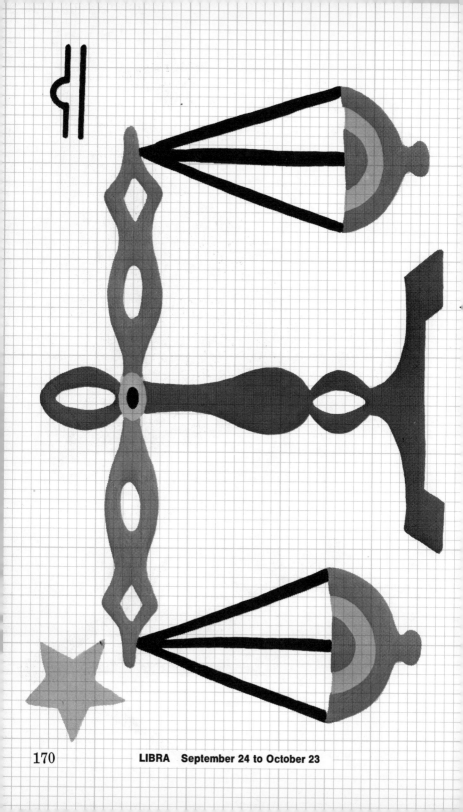

170   **LIBRA** **September 24 to October 23**

172

SAGITTARIUS   November 22 to December 21

CAPRICORN   December 22 to January 19

AQUARIUS   January 20 to February 18

PISCES   February 19 to March 20

175

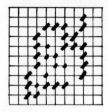

Sources

Listed here are retail and wholesale sources of needlepoint supplies—canvas, yarn, and other accessories. Some sources have catalogues for which there is sometimes a charge. Some send color cards and samples of wool and canvas on request. A few sell only their own designs. Contact the retail sources listed below for further information. Wholesale companies will deal only with retail sources and not with individual customers.

BARNES & BLAKE ART NEEDLEWORK, LTD., 148 East 28 St., New York, N.Y. 10016

BOUTIQUE MARGOT, 26 West 54 St., New York, N.Y. 10019

DESIREE DESIGN STUDIO FOR NEEDLECRAFTS, 7942 Wisconsin Ave., Suite 122, Bethesda, Md. 20014

T. E. DOELGER, Box 126, Blauvelt, N.Y. 10913

ENTRE NOUS, 1089 Post Road, Darien, Conn. 06820

FABRIC AND NOTION SHOP, 1335 Halstead Avenue, Mamaroneck, N.Y. 10543

FANCYWORK, 1235 First Ave., New York, N.Y. 10021

SUZY GIRARD, 1042 Lexington Ave., New York, N.Y. 10021

HAYSTACK, LTD., INC., 240 South Beverly Drive, Beverly Hills, Calif. 90212

FREDERICK HERRSCHNER CO., Hoover Road, Stevens Point, Wis. 54481

HILDE'S KNIT SHOP, 305 White Plains Road, Eastchester, N.Y. 10707

LUCY COOPER HILL, 1126 Kane Concourse, Bay Harbor Islands, Miami Beach, Fla. 33154

MILI HOLMES' STUDIO, 95 Colonial Road, New Canaan, Conn. 06840

IN STITCHES, 3901 Prairie Lane, Prairie Village, Kansas 66208

JEBBA, INC., 1208 San Julian St., Los Angeles, Calif. 90015

THE JEWELED NEEDLE, 920 Nicollet Mall, Minneapolis, Minn. 55402

THE KNITTING NEEDLE, Armonk, N.Y.

KATHARINE KNOX, 445 Plandome Road, Manhasset, N.Y. 11030

KRICK KITS, 61 Portland Drive, St. Louis, Mo. 63131

VIRGINIA MAXWELL CUSTOM NEEDLEWORK STUDIO, 3404 Kirby Drive, Houston, Texas 77006

ALICE MAYNARD, 558 Madison Ave., New York, N.Y. 10022

MAZALTOV'S, INC., 758 Madison Ave., New York, N.Y. 10020 and 1980 Union St., San Francisco, Calif. 94123

JEAN MC INTOSH, 1064 Valour Road, Winnipeg 10, Manitoba, Canada

B. J. MITCHELL, 928 Madison Ave., New York, N.Y. 10021

NANTUCKET NEEDLEWORKS, 11 South Water St., Nantucket Island, Mass. 02554

NEEDLECRAFT, 136 Chatsworth Ave., Larchmont, N.Y. 10538

NEEDLECRAFT HOUSE, West Townsend, Mass. 01474

THE NEEDLECRAFT SHOP, 13561 Ventura Boulevard, Sherman Oaks, Calif. 91403

NEEDLE NUTS, 3302 Mercer, Houston, Texas 77027

NEEDLEPOINT, INC., 2401 Magazine St., New Orleans, La. 70130

NEEDLEPOINT CORNER, 8121 Old York Road, Elkins Park, Pa. 19117

NEEDLEPOINT UNLIMITED, INC., P.O. Box 3051, Miami Beach, Fla. 33140

THE NEEDLE POINTS, 979 Third Ave., New York, N.Y. 10022

THE NEEDLEWORK STUDIO, INC., Bryn Mawr & Summit Grove Avenues, Bryn Mawr, Pa. 19010

NIMBLE FINGERS, INC., 283 Dartmouth St., Boston, Mass. 02116

THE NIMBLE THIMBLE, P.O. Box 713, Aptos, Calif. 95003

NINA NEEDLEPOINT, 860 Madison Ave., New York, N.Y. 10021

PAPILLON, Cates Plaza, 375 Pharr Road, N.E., Atlanta, Ga. 30305

PEACOCK ALLEY, 650 Croswell, S.E., Grand Rapids, Mich. 49506

THE QUARTER STITCH, 607 Dumaine St., New Orleans, La. 70116

MARGARET HAINES RANSOM, 229 Arbor Ave., West Chicago, Ill. 60185

SELMA'S ART NEEDLEWORK, 1645 Second Ave., New York, N.Y. 10028

THE SINKLER STUDIO, 336 King of Prussia Road, Box 93, Radnor, Pa. 19087

MONA SPOOR, 670 Undercliff Ave., Edgewater, N.J. 07020

THE STITCHERY, Wellesley, Mass. 02181

THE STUDIO, P.O. Box 7144, Kansas City, Mo. 64113

VALLEY HANDCRAFTERS, Avon Park, Avon, Conn. 06001

ERICA WILSON, INC., 40 East End Ave., New York, N.Y. 10028

THE WOOL FARM, 49 East 10 St., New York, N.Y. 10003

WOOLWORKS, 783 Madison Ave., New York, N.Y. 10021

FOR SPECIAL INFORMATION:

THE EMBROIDERERS' GUILD, Suite 228, 120 East 56 St., New York, N.Y. 10022. Literature and general information.

FREDERICK HERRSCHNER CO., Hoover Road, Stevens Point, Wis. 54481. Kapok-filled pillow forms in many sizes; dacron batting; rug backing.

MARTHA KLEIN, LTD., 3785 Broadway, New York, N.Y. 10032. Eyeglass cases, belts, telephone book covers, pillows, luggage straps, mountings, and frames for handbags.

PURSENALITIES, 1619 Grand Ave., Baldwin, N.Y. 11510. Handbag frames and handles.

WHOLESALE SOURCES

AA CREATIVE DESIGNS CO., 24 Chester Drive, Rye, N.Y. 10580

EMILE BERNAT & SONS, CO., 230 Fifth Ave., New York, N.Y. 10001. Yarns, No. 4 rug canvas, kits.

BRUNSWICK WORSTED MILLS, INC., 230 Fifth Ave., New York, N.Y. 10001. Canvas, yarn.

COATS & CLARK, INC., 430 Park Ave., New York, N.Y. 10022. Yarn.

COLUMBIA-MINERVA CORP., 295 Fifth Ave., New York, N.Y. 10010. Canvas, wool.

THE D.M.C. CORP., 107 Trumbull St., Elizabeth, N.J. 07206. Canvas, yarns.

DRITZ, SCOVILL MFG. CO., 350 Fifth Ave., New York, N.Y. 10001. Canvas, yarns.

ERIC GREENE & CO., 11144 Weddington St., Box 257, North Hollywood, Calif. 91603. Canvas, yarns.

HANDWORK TAPESTRIES, 3389 Colony Drive, Baldwin, L.I., N.Y. 11510. Canvas, yarns.

PARAGON ART & LINEN CO., INC., 385 Fifth Ave., New York, N.Y. 10016. Canvas, yarns.

PATERNAYAN BROTHERS, INC., 312 East 95 St., New York, N.Y. 10028. Canvas, yarns.

REYNOLDS INTERNATIONAL NEEDLEWORK GUILD, 160 Cabot St., West Babylon, N.Y. 11704. Canvas.

JOAN TOGGITT, LTD., 1170 Broadway, Room 406, New York, N.Y. 10001. Canvas, yarns, supplies, and instruction books.

BERNHARD ULLMAN CO., 30-20 Thomson Ave., Long Island City, N.Y. 11101. Canvas, yarn.

WILLIAM UNGER & CO., INC., 230 Fifth Ave., New York, N.Y. 10001. Bargello and needlepoint kits.

THE WILLIAMS MFG. CO., West Townsend, Mass. 01474. Canvas, yarns, accessories.

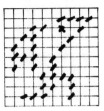

Index